The Covid Bounce

The Covid Bounce

Learning to Smile Again After the Pandemic

SUE BINDER, LPC

Jefferson, North Carolina

ISBN (print) 978-1-4766-8956-2 ♾
ISBN (ebook) 978-1-4766-4713-5

LIBRARY OF CONGRESS AND BRITISH LIBRARY
CATALOGUING DATA ARE AVAILABLE

Printed in the United States of America

Toplight is an imprint of McFarland & Company, Inc., Publishers

Box 611, Jefferson, North Carolina 28640
www.toplightbooks.com

To the medical couriers who traveled the roads
and highways throughout the pandemic,
transporting COVID tests to health departments
across the nation. They drove at risk of accident,
costs to their physical and mental health,
and the whims of Mother Nature.

Acknowledgments

A very special tribute to my wise editor and agent Alice Heiserman. Without her guidance and encouragement, this book would never have been completed. Alice has seen me successfully through three books, which would not have been printed without her red ink and editorial comments.

Susan Kilby, managing editor—development at McFarland, deserves special thanks, along with the entire editorial team.

I owe a special debt of gratitude to my entire behavioral health team at High Plains Community Health Center, who may have unknowingly contributed many ideas and suggestions to this book. Your support has made my work with patients rewarding, while providing much impetus for this book. Thank you, Sharon, Mary, Pauletta, Heather, Amber, Grace, and Sylvia.

Table of Contents

Preface

Monday, March 16, 2020.

I turn the key in my office door and lock it. I carry my laptop and a dozen manila folders with me. The material will be enough for me to work at home for a couple of days—just until this state of emergency has passed. Little did I know that I would never be returning to my office.

COVID-19 hit Colorado hard that day of March 16, 2020. Governor Jared Polis suspended dine-in services for restaurants and for other in-person operations. We marked the first of many deaths due to COVID that week. While the pandemic impacted other regions, Colorado had been spared to some extent. When two of my children phoned me that day and asked, "What are you doing at work?" and insisted, "You need to go home," I had a quick awakening to the spreading panic and exited my office at noon.

Perhaps it was my preoccupation with work that deterred me from being as attentive as I should have been to the creeping infection sweeping across the nation. I am a behavioral health therapist at a community health center. I carry a caseload of patients with a wide variety of diagnoses, including many on probation and under the supervision of child protective services.

I now found myself working at home off a TV tray. Initially, I missed the spacious office that I had carefully decorated upon my arrival at the clinic three years previously. The walls held plaques with positive quotes. My credentials hung on the wall. Books and music and therapeutic materials lined the shelves. Yet, as I began setting up my home office, I also was able to add inspirational photos, and I learned to appreciate modern technology. I viewed my patients online and conducted telephone sessions with them, and I discovered that I had fewer interruptions or distractions than when I was in my regular office. I learned that many of my patients also appreciated this process. With COVID about, all of us were isolated in our homes.

As I came to realize, working at home did not intimidate me. In fact, because of my personality, I embraced it. Others were angry, frightened, and resentful. The realization of how we met the pandemic differently led me to explore more fully just how we respond to crises in various manners.

Speaking with my editor and agent Alice Heiserman, I had the idea for a book on life after COVID. Together we began pursuing this topic. What were some key reactions? What individual and external fears drove the variety of responses? More importantly, how could people use the best of themselves to bounce back in a positive emotional, physical, and spiritual manner?

Like many others, I willingly gave up my office. I discovered that I am happy working at home, as are my current patients whom I visit virtually. Our early fears may now be lessened as we hope that the worst of COVID and its scourge may have passed. Yet, the ideas, suggestions, and tools within this book provide self-management methods for you to use on your journey to finding harmony and balance in your life at any time.

This book is written with an eye toward the end of the pandemic which will come gradually and unevenly from place to place. It expresses the point of view that that day, hopefully, will arrive in the near future when the acute danger has largely passed. This book is written for the reader looking beyond Covid and for anyone experiencing personal crises.

The pandemic and all other catastrophes and disasters in our lives are addressed well in the following quote by J.R.R. Tolkien:

> "I wish it need not have happened in my time," said Frodo.
> "So do I," said Gandalf, "and so do all who live to see such times. But that is not for them to decide. All we have to decide is what to do with the time that is given us."

Section I—The Impact of COVID

1

Reactions and Responses

Did you breeze through the pandemic with few adjustments to your lifestyle? Perhaps you worked from home and enjoyed the solitude. You met with your co-workers online. Overall, you didn't mind the disruptions to routine brought about by COVID-19. You adjusted very well and carved out your new schedule. You were comfortable and even felt a sense of contentment. When you did have to go out, you donned your mask and kept your distance. You sanitized your doorknobs and cabinets. Overall, this pandemic thing did not seem so bad.

And just when you felt like you were thriving under your routine, along came Moderna, Pfizer, Johnson & Johnson. Suddenly, these wonderful vaccines impacted your personal, occupational, and social existence. The normal that you had come to appreciate faded as people and some businesses dropped mask restrictions.

Now you could attend in-person meetings again. You could sit with 15,000 other fans through your favorite baseball game, and you could browse without fear through the mall and the nearest big box store. For many of your family, friends, and co-workers, the news was terrific. But for you, all the extra stimuli, the noise, the sights, and the sounds, felt overwhelming. By limiting social contact, you knew you also could manage any regulations around COVID variants.

For others, the lifting of restrictions brought a sense of relief, of excitement, of a return to their normal schedules. Many could not wait to rejoin their work crew, participate in team meetings, and plan for company parties. Some families rejoiced as airlines opened up, and they traveled across the country to reunions and celebrated in grand style all the missed events of the past two years. Then came the announcement that COVID had developed a new strain, known as the Delta variant. They felt their frustration rise, hoping that their activities would not be impacted. They questioned the necessity of the vaccine, even when they learned certain restrictions would be applied to group gatherings.

A third group of people had mixed responses to the pandemic. At first, they may have been upset and angry over having to leave their workplace and don a mask to buy groceries. Yet, at other times they may have felt pleased to be at home with their family, away from the continual interaction with co-workers and office politics. Their responses waffled back and forth. They were often content with the current situation, but at other times they felt frustrated and annoyed. Their reactions and behaviors varied, depending on their views, perhaps sometimes influenced by daily news broadcasts.

Not surprisingly, some people reacted to the pandemic with fear and anger, even taking to social media to express their negative views. Others were able to manage well, actually experiencing personal growth. Finally, some fluctuated in their responses, sometimes angry and frustrated and, at other times, enjoying time with family, friends, television, and games, almost akin to going on a vacation.

Indeed, we are all different in our responses to situations, personal or pandemic. Epictetus, the Greek philosopher, may have said it best when he wrote, "People are not upset by things themselves, but by what they tell themselves about those things." As individuals, we told ourselves many different stories about COVID-19, depending on our personalities, the use of our senses, and our life experiences. Our interpretations of the pandemic itself, the way the authorities and government managed it, and the personal impact revealed much about ourselves.

We're human. Our perceptions and interpretations of any event can vary greatly from person to person. Arguments evolve. Misunderstandings arise. Relationships dissolve over how we interpret situations. COVID-19 slammed like an asteroid into our lives, disrupting all our routines, our "normals," our everyday way of life. It created havoc, hoarding, and fear for many.

While readjusting to a new world, many of us lost our safety nets. We each had our interpretations of reality, of the messages we fed ourselves about the events. Our reactions were many and varied, largely dependent upon what we chose to tell ourselves and believe about the pandemic. Do I really need to sanitize all my doorknobs and my kitchen shelves daily, and what about the food I just purchased from the store? What is the correct method of washing my hands to avoid any infection? Is this the end of the world or just a hoax? Is it safe to get a vaccine?

Whatever your response has been, it's important to accept that your feelings were natural under the circumstances. Viktor E. Frankl, author and survivor of the Holocaust, stated, "An abnormal reaction to an abnormal situation is normal behavior." Your feelings and perceptions were based on your personality, management style, and past life experiences. Therefore, it's understandable that some individuals had reactions totally different from what you experienced. They also may have a completely different response to readjusting to life after COVID. Recognizing those varying responses, your actions, and your emotions during the pandemic provides a powerful key to your healthy journey back to a state of contentment.

Personality Responses

When you were sent home to work, did you smile at the thought of fewer interruptions by people in the office? Once you set up your home office, did you feel more in control, better organized, less anxious? Did you often feel that you preferred being alone where you could concentrate more effectively on tasks? A person with this personality type is labeled an **introvert**. Typically, introverts enjoy spending time alone. They need this time to rest and recharge their batteries and often prefer interaction with only one or two people instead of groups. This is not necessarily a negative trait because introverts hold many high personal qualities. They are often organized, thoughtful, excellent planners. Here's more good news. If you see yourself as an introvert, you may have fared well throughout the pandemic. Content at home, studying, reading, embracing hobbies, watching TV, listening to music, and, yes, in many cases, working—sometimes even more intensely and longer than in your regular office.

However, it also explains why you may be feeling overwhelmed by any post–COVID changes. More people, more in-person meetings. More cars on the highway, traffic jams. Out of the twenty-five types of cereal lining the shelf, which do you choose? More of everything pelting you.

These introverted traits will carry you through as you integrate back into the traditional workplace. Your ability to study and focus, along with your characteristics and strengths of resilience and planning, will aid your progress as you integrate new tools for growth.

You may know others who felt jolted by the pandemic. The loss of contact with their co-workers and family may have overwhelmed them. When they could not attend ball games, graduations and birthdays, their resentment and anger may have spun out of control.

These individuals may have felt isolated. Their home may have suddenly felt like a prison cell where they were confined for well over a year. If you fit in this category, the loss of your social network may have seemed intolerable. People who exhibit these characteristics are often known as **extroverts**. Extroverts typically enjoy spending time with others and dislike being alone. They generally enjoy crowds and parties, and the quality time spent with others helps them rejuvenate. If this is your primary trait, you may also be outgoing and more talkative.

The good news is that you are a people person. You interact with others with confidence, easily share, and can create new friendships. This trait benefits you professionally and personally and will benefit you as you continue reshaping your life after COVID. The transition back may be much less difficult for you than for some of your cohorts.

However, in a rush to re-establish social connections and rejuvenate your energy, you can overdo it. You may tend to relive your earlier years by over socializing, attending extravagant parties, concerts and entertainment events, and eating and drinking too much. Readjusting to a more stable way of managing your daily activities to enjoy the newfound freedom and maintain personal responsibilities is vital, and you can self-manage. You will be able to bounce back from COVID and its variants by using the tools and skills inside these chapters.

People who display a third type of personality often managed very well during the pandemic. They are often termed **ambiverts**. If you fit this category, you may be very adept at handling your emotions, enjoying the break from people and binging on your favorite TV series. Yet, at other times, you may become restless, frustrated, wanting to party with friends.

This ability to perceive the benefits and the drawbacks of the pandemic meant that you managed with less fallout. When the media reports recommended wearing a mask, you probably did so. When the news said it wasn't necessary, you shrugged your shoulders and complied. This ability to flex may have significantly aided you as you began bouncing back from COVID.

On the other hand, you may struggle at times with your own decisions, wondering if it would really be safe to shop without a mask now or still questioning if COVID wasn't just a conspiracy. Ambiverts may benefit from using the tools and suggestions within this book to aid them in developing specific goals to establish more stability with their readjustment to life without COVID. If you fit this description, be patient with yourself as you locate new methods of managing your emotional needs.

As you read through these various personality types, you may have noted how differently some responded to the pandemic. They also responded very differently when the pandemic appeared to have dissipated with the arrivals of vaccines—even with COVID variants. Then they demonstrated other responses when federal, state, and business mandates were announced. Hopefully, you can recognize and accept that it is okay if people perceive events differently. The key factor is that you accept your responses and develop tools to overcome the excessive stimuli you now experience.

Life Experiences

Personality styles have been formed by many variables, most notably your life experiences. For example, if you were born into adversity or into a disruptive and chaotic family system, or if your parents divorced or one parent was never in the home, these will have affected how you interpret events. Perhaps your environment was filled with alcohol or drug use with constant arguing and fighting present. As a child, you may have almost raised yourself or your siblings. You may have felt invisible or that no one loved you. You lost your sense of trust in yourself and the world around you. You may have fallen into criminal behavior, spending time behind bars. All this adversity and lack of a support system affected you and how you responded to the pandemic.

Maybe you came from a family system that coped well with adversity. They were supportive, and even when disagreements arose, they managed to solve problems in a calm, respectful manner. There were rules, and, yes, you were disciplined when you disobeyed. But you were not physically beaten. You felt loved, even if your parents split up. You may have had a few slips along the way, a few traffic tickets, and maybe you drank beer or tried a joint or two, but basically, you avoided drugs and learned to manage most of your problems with the support of family and friends. This upbringing led you to a more positive and trusting view of life. As a result, you were able to manage the pandemic months reasonably well.

Your life experiences, whether positive or negative, have impacted your responses to the pandemic and other events in your life. For example, your exposure to fearful situations may have triggered extreme reactions and created long-lasting phobias.

Phobia and Fear Responses

Our personality and our personal history certainly can affect our responses and reactions to events and adversity. However, one shared factor during the pandemic dominated the landscape—fear. The pandemic brought forth exaggerated or irrational fears that many of us did not realize existed. Some of us already carried extreme and specific fears based on life experiences, brain chemistry, and genetics. The word *phobia* comes from the Greek word *phóbos*, meaning aversion, fear or morbid fear; this condition is an anxiety disorder. A diagnosis requires that the symptoms be present for more than six months and include a rapid onset of fear, out of proportion to the immediate danger. Such fears result in an overpowering need for people to avoid anything that triggers their anxiety.

There are three primary types of phobias. The first, specific or simple phobias, are linked to an identifiable cause that may not occur daily, such as a fear of snakes, dogs or spiders, the dark, or heights.

Many of these are caused by an early childhood event. They do not generally create significant or ongoing or daily disturbances in a person's behavior.

The second social phobia or anxiety is a profound fear of public humiliation or being judged by others. The idea of large social gatherings is terrifying for those people. They will go out of their way to avoid such situations, and if exposed to them, they can exhibit fear and anxiety.

The third, agoraphobia, is much more intense and can result in people being fearful of using public transportation, being in open or enclosed places, standing in line or being in a crowd or simply being outside of the home.

During the initial stages of COVID-19, I knew a man who had already been diagnosed with agoraphobia. The pandemic made his experience even more unbearable. He would not step outside his house, even to walk in the yard. Others had to bring him food. He began to deteriorate to the point that his family had to obtain mental health services to intervene due to his tendencies toward suicide.

People with social phobia or agoraphobia find it much harder to avoid triggers. They are inevitably bombarded with people when purchasing groceries. They cannot avoid others when entering an elevator. They can begin organizing their life around avoiding the cause of their fear. They may experience abnormal breathing, accelerated heartbeat, sweating, hot flashes, chest pains, nausea, dizziness or even confusion. I know individuals who went to the emergency room, convinced they had a heart attack when the cause was their fears.

Some phobias may have affected people even more intensely during the pandemic, such as claustrophobia, the fear of being in constricted or confined spaces, or hypochondria, the fear of becoming ill. When people have several combined phobias known as *complex phobias,* the management becomes even more difficult. Finally, with the introduction of vaccines, another significant phobia arose—the fear of blood, injury, and injection (BII). This particular fear may have contributed to some people resisting or refusing vaccinations.

With dozens of identified phobias, it is little wonder that the list continues to grow. One of the newest is nomophobia, the fear of being without a cell phone or computer, also identified as the fear of being without or out of touch with technology.

Researchers note that phobias are often linked to the "fight or flight" hormones, putting our minds and bodies in an anxious or stressed state. The brain recalls events that have been dangerous or possibly deadly in our lives, and when we are faced with those triggers, we react with the same anxiety. For example, a child whose parents wanted to teach him to swim tossed him in a river, where he almost drowned. In their zeal to help their child learn to swim, the parents may have instilled a fear of water which became a phobia.

Phobias are treatable. Speaking to a psychologist or psychiatrist can reduce fears and anxiety symptoms and help people manage their reactions to specific phobias. At times, a provider may prescribe medication to aid in the anxiety and mood symptoms. Several therapeutic approaches may be helpful. Along with traditional cognitive behavioral therapy (CBT) and dialectical behavioral treatment (DBT), other methods that may be effective include desensitization and reprocessing (EMDR), virtual reality therapy, and hypnotherapy. The use of any therapeutic technique should be under the guidance of a licensed and trained therapist.

When phobias are joined with our personality styles and life experiences, it is small wonder that we can each view and manage our reactions and responses differently. COVID-19 brought fear to the surface in a multitude of ways: fear of sickness, death, being lied to, the end of days, contamination, and a barrage of conspiracy theories. Even for those who held characteristics and histories that enabled them to balance their reactions to events in a healthy manner, fear still invaded their lives. Fear appeared like a mantra on the daily news broadcasts, spilling over to our nightly dinner tables.

Most often, we do not recognize fear at its initial arrival. After all, what is fear? How can we best define it? For clarity, I define fear as an adaptive emotion that mobilizes energy so we can deal with a potential or personal threat. When that occurs, the brain produces both physical and mental changes, and the reaction can interfere with our decision-making and our sense of safety. For example, if a truck propelled down the highway straight at you, you might begin trembling, your heart might beat rapidly, and you might find yourself crying or screaming. Later, you might experience anxiety, be unable to sleep, feel depressed, or even experience nightmares.

In this instance, fear serves as protection. It ensures our survival. Next time you're on the highway, you may drive a little more slowly and be certain your seat belt is buckled. Fear keeps us from taking dangerous risks. You may have decided to get vaccinated against the possibility of getting COVID or one of the variants.

Fear also acts upon many triggers. For example, if we feel a loss of control over our lives, such as caused by COVID, that can create fear. If we feel rejected or unimportant in our relationships with others, that can result in fear. Finally, fear can be triggered by feeling unimportant, guilty or ashamed or by an inability to manage ourselves. This type of fear can create anger, irritation and even violence in some cases. These emotions can then be outwardly directed to others, often a spouse or children. In the case of the pandemic, we might have blamed the Centers for Disease Control (CDC), another country, the government, our neighbors or other entities.

Fear can stifle our ability to reshape our life after the pandemic. Fear can push us into reactive thinking so that we are scared to achieve, unable to follow up on job opportunities or keep important medical appointments. For example, after being on lockdown for many months, just putting your key in the ignition of your car for the first time may make your stomach quiver. Facing the meat counter with a dozen different types of hamburger can feel overpowering, even nauseating.

But don't forget that fear can also propel you in a positive direction. Fear can push us to succeed, to perform, to go beyond our capabilities. During the pandemic, many essential workers in the medical field, medical couriers, and social workers continued to report to work when they felt exhausted because they felt the danger and fear that COVID could infect their communities. This same fear can also propel us into a positive reconstruction of our lives. It can lead us to recognize that hamburger choices are insignificant in the larger scheme of life.

Natural Reactions

How you make your hamburger selection can depend upon how your brain generates responses to a threat or to fear. The natural reactions to danger include **fight, flee**, or **freeze**. Fear generates hormonal and physiological changes. Take a look at your responses. How did you react when you first learned of COVID? Examining your reactions is important because it illustrates how you manage your life without a mask, without restrictions. More importantly, your pattern indicates how to make a healthy, long-lasting readjustment to life beyond COVID.

Fight may have been the initial response by many people to the pandemic. Perhaps they argued with others, even family, about the validity of the disease. Or they may have questioned the validity of the Centers for Disease Control's (CDC) findings and recommendations. Maybe they fought mask-wearing. Distancing seemed silly, unnecessary. But they may have seemed to have no conscious control over this automatic reaction.

You may have wanted to **flee**. Stay away from the grocery store. No medical or dental appointments. Wherever people gathered, you stayed away. The safest action was to lock yourself in your residence to avoid illness or death. Again, you pursued one type of response to survival. For you, your response now to the opening up of grocery stores and restaurants may be frightening. How do you enter a building with tables full of unmasked people, chattering a mile a minute? Even though you've been vaccinated, you still have a strong desire to block the sound with your earplugs.

Other people simply **froze**. Uncertain whether it was safe to visit family, to attend ball games or to shop, you may have hesitated, remained uncertain, making no significant changes. You remained as you were, content to ruminate on the pandemic, waiting for more information. You locked yourself into your comfort zone, and, despite the events going on in the outside world, you remained as closely aligned to your own "normal" as possible.

These varied responses determined how various individuals managed during the COVID-19 pandemic. More importantly, they will determine to a large degree how you are now readjusting your life—and how you continue to shape a new, improved version of yourself. Using some of the suggestions and tools in this book, you can successfully overcome your fears and navigate the journey forward, regardless of your personality style.

Mental Health Influences

COVID-19's impact is much more complicated than our personalities and life experiences that have aroused our fears. These factors have also significantly impacted our mental health. Some individuals came into the pandemic already diagnosed with emotional problems, which may have further impacted them during the weeks of uncertainty. Some people who had no known mental health issues may have been driven by anxiety attacks or bouts of depression. Others who suffered from past traumatic events may have had their symptoms further triggered by the COVID outbreak and, as a result, experienced more severe trauma.

The purpose of mentioning the pandemic's effect on mental health is to acknowledge the importance of treatment and therapy during and following the outbreak. If you have recovered from COVID yourself, you may be experiencing mental health after-effects. Those who already have medical and behavioral health providers are encouraged to continue treatment with them. Those who still feel anxiety, depression, rage, anger, or confusion may have suffered from the inability to sleep or are overeating or not eating enough or are addicted to alcohol or drugs. These individuals should use their support system and professional help. Others who have been diagnosed with more significant disorders such as forms of bipolar disorder, schizophrenia or borderline personality disorder should seek out a licensed psychiatrist.

Perhaps you had moments or days during the past months when you felt sad or depressed. Perhaps you sometimes felt so stressed that you wanted to throw your coffee cup at the wall. These emotions are understandable. As restrictions lifted, you may have felt even more anxiety, especially with the arrival of COVID variants. Some people were still wearing masks. Am I supposed to? Is it safe? I just want to stay home, but I need to shop. But when I walk into the store, they play loud music. People talk everywhere I turn and block the aisle, which is almost worse than being locked down.

Who wouldn't be confused with all these mixed messages? Allow yourself to have these feelings. Accept them. However, if they continue unchecked, if you don't bounce back within a few days, please reach out for help.

How to find support can be a challenge. First of all, look to your closest friends or family members. Pick up the phone and chat. Tell them how you are feeling. Vent your emotions. Chances are they are feeling exactly like you. Just knowing that others are in the same situation can give you that sense that you are okay. No, you are not crazy. It's the world that has gone crazy!

If you are depressed or your feelings of anxiety persist, contact a local behavioral or mental health provider. You can check listings on your computer for the closest licensed counselors, therapists, social workers, or psychiatrists. These professionals have been trained to listen to your concerns and offer tools to aid you in managing your emotions and, yes, fears. They can also conduct simple screenings to determine any diagnoses and appropriate treatment.

During COVID, many professionals did not meet with their clients in person, but agencies, hospitals, and clinics were awarded funding to cover tele-visits. That meant that you could talk with your doctor or therapist by telephone and, often, by video calls via Zoom, Spruce, and other applications. This wonderful technology allowed these professionals to observe their clients' body language and physical responses. Many of these same professionals are continuing with tele-visits because they realize that this communication method is very convenient for many of their patients, especially those who live at a distance or are disabled.

For some people, their symptoms might have accelerated to the point where they felt out of control. They may have fallen into a despondent state where nothing seemed to lift their feelings. They could find no pleasure in being with their family, sharing good food, or enjoying nature. Everything sucks! At some point, they may have thought the world was coming to an end anyway, so what the hell! If you hear a friend or family member speak this way, take it seriously. Do not brush it off as "having a bad day." Instead, call for help. You can call the police, the emergency number in your community, or a mental health professional. You might reason that your friend will never speak to you again. Please take that chance. Make that call.

During the COVID-19 pandemic, some thought that there might be an increase in suicides. Statistics are inconsistent as to how many suicides can be directly attributed to the pandemic during that time frame. There are many variables associated with self-harm.

With COVID, the economic impact may prove to be a prime consideration. However, social interactions, family cohesiveness, or medical problems may account for some suicidal thoughts and actions.

Being aware of your own emotions and the feelings of others was never more critical than during the pandemic. Looking out for your family, friends, and neighbors was never more important. But do not forget self-care. Perhaps even now, you have said, "I'm fine" or "I'm good" when you really did not feel fine or good. Do not feel shy about reaching out. Think about your reactions during the past months. Then consider how you are feeling now. Did you feel a sense of relief that it was all over until the announcement of the variants and increasing hospital numbers? Or are you still struggling with the fallout and wondering how to adjust to an ever-changing world?

What did you tell yourself about the pandemic? Were you fearful of getting a vaccine? Did you finally get one version, but were you fearful that it might not be totally effective? Did you decide not to get one? What are you telling yourself about the days ahead? Remember, it's not the events themselves but how you reacted to them that determines your emotions. Hopefully, this book will provide some ideas, inspiration, and tools to aid you as you bounce back from COVID-19.

2

Kids and COVID

As adults, we responded to the initial announcement of COVID-19 with various personality traits and characteristics. Regardless of our personal fears and views of the pandemic, we managed to go on with our days. We may have returned to work when our company cleared us to come back. Perhaps we lost our job. Or perhaps we were fortunate enough to be able to work from home. As the virus continued its expansion, we continued with our daily routines, and with the addition of the vaccines, we may have breathed a sigh of relief. At least for the moment, there appeared to be a reprieve. Then came the Delta and Omicron variants, and cases began to rise again in some parts of the country. Still, we persevered.

But we are adults, somehow able to process the events and the ever-changing landscape and retain a sense of normalcy in our lives. But what about the kids? What about our children? How did they manage during all those months, and how are they managing now? Those under twelve were ineligible to get the vaccine, so in 2021 there were a large number of new cases of COVID. And how were and are they affected emotionally? As parents and caregivers, we do not want to overlook the impact on our children.

Our children may have mirrored our responses. Children are very imitative. If you reacted with fear, anger, skepticism, outrage, or a shrug of your shoulders, these actions could be reflected in how your children saw the pandemic and how they managed their emotions and the disruptions in their lives.

During the COVID pandemic, children were impacted by the problems that faced their parents, including isolation, childcare, and finances. Some parents could not pay their bills and are now being evicted from their homes. In addition, schools were initially closed, cutting off children's interaction with their friends, and most of them experienced a loss of their regular learning environment. As a result, they learned or used new visual programs and interacted with their teachers through technology. Of course, adjusting to such a new learning environment was especially difficult for children with special needs or younger children who could not sit still in front of their televisions or computers for the length of the school day.

The list of extra problems brought on by COVID is extensive.

Health: Children get meals, including breakfast and lunch, in many districts. Some schools continued to provide meals, but parents had to drive once or twice per day to pick up the meals, and many parents were unable to pick up meals for lack of transportation. For other children, the loss of school meals meant not having access to nourishing meals. Consequently, many pediatricians found a growing obesity epidemic among children exacerbated by the lack of school breakfast and lunch programs.

"With the school year in full swing, product shortfalls, delivery delays and labor shortages have pushed the nation's public school meal programs to a crisis point. It's the same economic forces plaguing other industries. Still, the stakes are higher: Many low-income American children get the majority of their nutrition from school meals," according to an article in the *Washington Post* (Reiley, 2021). So, even though many kids are back at school, the problems continue.

Mental Health: School counselors are present to listen, to catch serious problems that may be occurring in the home, such as domestic violence, abuse, and neglect. Ordinarily, teachers would spot some troubling issues, but with tele-learning, they could not be the witnesses, and many kids fell through the cracks.

Social interaction: We all had less interaction with friends, and our ability to generate new friends in an online environment was difficult and, for some, impossible, especially where computer services were limited or unavailable.

Self-esteem: Loss of activities, such as sports, hobbies and clubs, meant many people felt great loneliness.

Medical access: Many medical and mental health providers had limited access. If children were already engaged in therapy, they might have experienced a gap in progress for several months.

As a result of these disruptions, parents have reported[1] that their children exhibited increased irritability, clinginess and fear and problems with appetite and sleep during the pandemic. These feelings can persist even into adulthood and affect how children manage disasters and make the usual decisions and outcomes in their day-to-day lives as adults.

Children living with an abusive or substance-abusing adult may have felt a measure of comfort in attending school each day. School provided an escape for them, a safety net. They may have felt that someone there—a teacher or social worker—cared about them, that they were not alone in their emptiness and fears. Schools have provided supportive services and trained individuals to spot mental health issues in children.

At least at the beginning of the pandemic, children were forced to adapt to different ways of learning. My daughter, who teaches second graders, reports the struggles she and her students experienced while learning new tools in a different atmosphere. Parents struggled to help their children learn these programs, but their skills were often limited too. Children frequently were able to help their parents. Home also provided many interruptions to their learning. Often there was little separation of the learning area from family areas, with little brothers and sisters around, parents arguing—all interfered with the normal classroom learning.

Parents who displayed different learning styles and personality characteristics played an enormous role in how learning took place. The parent who exhibited extrovert traits may have felt overwhelmed by the intrusion in their life and cursed and yelled at the pandemic in front of the children. They may have felt trapped without their usual social interaction. The children witnessed these reactions and may have displayed such frustration themselves.

The parent who calmly adjusted to the early pandemic also affected their child with their easy-going "I'm on vacation" manner. But keep in mind that children have their own personalities, and, for some parents, this attitude may have backfired, making

---

1. Singh, Shweta, et al. 2020. "Impact of COVID-19 and Lockdown on Mental Health of Children and Adolescents: A Narrative Review with Recommendations." *Psychiatry Research* 293 (November). https://www.sciencedirect.com/science/article/pii/S016517812031725X?via%3Dihub.

the child disrespect their parent who doesn't stand up to the "system."

Several parents reported that their children didn't want to go back to school when the pandemic eased. They were used to the more relaxed atmosphere, and the idea of having to wear a mask to a class created open rebellion. Other children couldn't wait to jump back into the classroom and return to choir practice and the book fair.

As the pandemic appeared to dissipate, schools reopened, but the arrival of the Delta variant meant that schools had to review their teaching approach, mask policies and quarantine measures. Different school districts took varying approaches, largely dependent upon the age of the students and the decisions of local school boards.

We don't yet know the full effect of COVID on children, either from the initial stages or as it altered its course. However, we do know that some children have managed much better and will continue to thrive. When children live in a safe, stable and nurturing environment with their family and community, they stand a much better chance of bouncing back from adversity and catastrophe.

Regardless of their personality traits, parents and caregivers can take many helpful steps to ensure that their children continue to thrive after the pandemic and any other outbreaks or fearful events.

Watch your reactions: As safety valves for our children, you need to keep your stress level down. As you move through this book, examine some of the mindfulness and calming tools that can aid you, regardless of the stage of COVID, to control your anxiety.

Stay connected: Allow your child to make that phone call to a friend, write e-mails and perhaps do a craft using video with a friend.

Remember personal care: Remind yourself and your child to take time for relaxation tools, such as reading or coloring or maybe watching a movie.

Encourage talk: Let your child know (at any age) that they can ask questions and talk about their fears. I have provided on my website colorful photos depicting a wide variety of emotions for younger children as an adjunct to encouraging sharing, which aids them in pointing out the feelings they are experiencing.

Teach prevention: Simple health tips, such as washing hands properly, covering coughs, and keeping germs out of our bodies, are necessary all the time, not just during a pandemic. During COVID and variants, this includes proper use of their mask. I find it works well to ask, "Who is your favorite superhero?" followed by "How does he keep strong and healthy to fight the bad people?"

Have family time: Set aside time to play games together, cook a meal together, exercise together, and laugh. Have fun. Having fun together provides a bond for our children and gives them a sense of protection.

Keep informed: As parents, keep yourself informed as the pandemic alters its course. When is it safe to go out without a mask? Is your child at a safe age for vaccinations? Are there positive cases at their school?

These tips can help build resilience in your children. Kids can spring back from a lot of disruptions if they have solid foundations at home. Children who live with violence and discord in their homes experience much more difficulty adjusting to life events. Their ability to self-manage, especially their emotions, can be damaged. As a result, they may turn to drugs and other addictions to stifle their feelings as they develop. They may take a detour that leads them to crime, to jail, and to prison.

Many mental health conditions develop by the time children reach their teens. Children may experience dire loneliness, believe no one cares, and feel sad, depressed, hopeless, angry, and even suicidal. If early problems, including any associated with the pandemic, are not addressed, they can continue into adulthood and affect future quality of life.

Adolescents experienced significant upheaval in their lives during the COVID pandemic with its fluctuations. With a driving need to assert their independence, they engage in activities that often try the limits of their caregivers under ordinary circumstances. Combine that with their risk-taking and rebellious streaks. They faced a challenge that perhaps was more traumatic than their elders.

As the pandemic shutdown began, their schools were shut down, and they were isolated from the daily interaction with their friends. Perhaps that senior boy had just begun a romance with the girl across the aisle in his homeroom. He had visions of asking her to the prom, but those dreams have now vanished. No romance—no prom. His goal of scoring the home run at the next ball game is also gone. Forget homecoming, and there would be no graduation this year. This physical distancing interfered with their routine and resulted in frustration, anger, and lingering depression.

Many adolescents missed out on their mental health, speech therapy, and occupational health services with school closures. Of course, they also missed out on life events such as birthdays, family reunions, and funerals. Many teenagers who held jobs were initially impacted with a job loss and the resultant lack of income. As the pandemic leveled out, some restaurants opened to carry-out or pick-up orders only but work hours often had been cut. Hit financially, teens often felt isolated and out of control. Their families were struggling to pay the light bill, and they could not help. Many adolescents had little support or security in their own homes.

The home environment further complicated their adjustment to COVID. Often, teens had parents and caregivers who used alcohol or drugs, yelled, threw dishes across the room, and physically struck each other, profoundly affecting how they viewed the pandemic. These are homes with no support for a child's education or health and homes that denied the existence of COVID and shrugged off the need for vaccinations, even when the pandemic eased. The witnessing of home violence, combined with the pandemic, left some adolescents traumatized. They were impacted physically, emotionally, and socially.

With the raging hormones in their brains, teenagers experience additional pressure. Recent research has shown that the human brain circuitry is not mature until one's early twenties. The last connections are the links between the prefrontal cortex, the seat of judgment and problem-solving and emotional center in the limbic system, especially the amygdala, an almond-shaped cluster of nuclei located inside the cerebral hemisphere, where it plays a crucial role in our memory, decision-making, and emotions, including anxiety, depression, and fear responses.

As a result, teens find it more difficult to interrupt an action underway, think before acting, and choose between safer and riskier alternatives. Their judgment can be overwhelmed by the urge for new experiences, thrill-seeking, and sexual and aggressive impulses. Resisting social pressure is also more difficult for teens than for older people.

The adolescent brain is reshaped beginning at puberty. The reward system, where addictive drugs and romantic love develops, expands. The brain is pouring out adrenal stress hormones, sex hormones, and growth hormones, which influence the emotions and behaviors present in teens. Small wonder that many teens develop high levels of depression and anxiety during and after the pandemic. Studies show that any pandemic, especially the current one, also causes worry, feelings of helplessness, and social and risky behaviors among children and adolescents.

As a result, teenagers can take unhealthy detours in their lives, such as substance abuse, suicide attempts, relationship problems, pregnancy, academic issues, and absenteeism from work. Isolated at home, they may spend a lot of time on electronic devices, leading to risky and dangerous conversations with unsavory people. It can lead to relationship problems with friends and family and a failure to be productive. The importance of healthy conversations with our teens is critical. Establishing a secure environment and routine with safety nets in place goes a long way toward preventing impulsive and dangerous behaviors.

Regardless of the child's age, it is extremely important to get help if you spot unhealthy symptoms in your child. What resources are available?

School counselors: Many schools are now operating as before the pandemic. Turn to the trained counselor. Most of these are professionals with specialized training for helping students. They can set up sessions with your children and, if needed, refer them to a mental health provider. They may also have tests to evaluate the child's needs further.

Resources are available to help school counselors who also may be adjusting to the challenges of the pandemic. The American Counseling Association (ACA) has a resource hub where information about the pandemic with telehealth tips and self-care practices is provided. In addition, the American School Counselor Association contains valuable information related to reentry and the school counselor's role. These tools can be found at https:online.tamiu.ed/articles/education/school-counseling-post-vocie.aspx.

Child behavioral health professionals: These therapists are specialists in children's emotional needs. They understand stages of development and also have instruments for testing the child's emotions further. They can also make referrals to psychiatrists or other treatment professionals or centers if needed.

Members of the clergy: Your local spiritual or religious leader can provide calming tools, a listening ear, and daily devotions and prayer suggestions. They may also have training in therapy and various techniques that you can verify with them. They, too, can make appropriate referrals if needed.

Due to the pandemic, the importance of children's mental health has led to several bills in Congress. The COVID-19 Mental Health Research Act proposed research on pandemic-related mental health impacts, including children and adolescents, but it is still languishing in committee. In my state, the Rapid Mental Health Response for Colorado Youth bill establishes a temporary program allowing youth to access mental health and substance use disorder services for free or reduced costs. The American Rescue Plan Act allocates funding for pediatric care access and youth suicide prevention. The American Jobs Plan and American Families Plan include upgrades in school and nutrition programs.

The development of such programs reflects a recognition that our children have been profoundly affected by the pandemic. It also recognizes that our children may continue to experience adverse symptoms for many years. While these programs are certainly needed, the key to aiding our children on their journey toward resilience and stability lies within parents and caregivers.

Whatever your personality trait—introvert, extrovert, ambivert—or whatever your history, fears, or comfort zones, one thing is necessary: helping your children and yourself bounce back from COVID. You will benefit from taking a close look at how significantly the pandemic affected you—and your mind.

3

Effects on the Mind

The pandemic has damaged your mind. You may not want to hear this. You may believe that's a ridiculous statement. After all, aren't you still the same you? Aren't you the person with the same characteristics, beliefs, personality, and fears that you held before COVID struck its mighty blow?

That's what you want to believe. But let's look at the reality. You were subjected to a bombardment of information. Television news, Facebook, e-mails, tweets, streams galore. Some of this information you agreed with. Some you found nasty, disagreeable. Some you ignored. Some you bought into 100 percent. Which information is correct? Which data is misleading? Does some of it collide with your spiritual or religious beliefs?

When you step aside and review your personal history since November 2019, what do you find? Remember, no one knows you like you. Have you been confused at times? Have you felt overwhelmed? Have you questioned the reality of the pandemic? Did I really have to wear a mask? Weren't my rights being violated? Maybe you even had disagreements with family and friends. Guess what? It's okay if you have had such thoughts. Maybe you even felt frustrated and angry at times.

Surely, you still shouldn't be feeling this way! Yet, as you consider what troubling thoughts and changes are racing through your mind, you might admit that you still hold a measure of fear with the advent of COVID variables. Perhaps it is a different kind of fear, but it is real. Consider picking up your car keys for the first time in fifteen months when you haven't even thought about filling the gas tank or getting an oil change. Yes, you are excited, and a part of you is pleased with this newfound freedom, but your hands are shaky. Acknowledging those feelings is okay and valuable to adjusting beyond COVID.

Yes, recognizing that your brain has been through a huge upheaval is extremely important to reshaping yourself. Facing any fears you have, shoving aside any personal antagonism, and moving to a gentler and more accepting self is vital to change.

The brain is our CPU unit. It serves as our central operating system for both physical and emotional responses. The limbic system, the autonomic nervous system and the reticular activating system all interact to aid us in processing emotions. Specifically, the portion known as the amygdala plays an enormous role in emotions, such as anxiety and depression, in both humans and animals, especially in the area of fear-based memories.

When we examine the role of fear, for example, associated with trauma, the impact on the brain is significant. People who have experienced serious injuries or sexual violence, witnessed violence, or participated in or witnessed war may develop symptoms associated with the accompanying fear surrounding the event. Those fears can persist in nightmares, flashbacks, anxiety attacks, hypervigilance and paranoia. They can impact memory and cause an exaggerated startle response. These are symptoms of posttraumatic stress disorder (PTSD).

We all react differently to trauma, depending upon the type and the personal impact. There is no right or wrong way to respond. Trauma can result from one-time events, like COVID. It can also result from ongoing or repeated stress, such as domestic violence or childhood neglect. Other contributing factors might include surgery, a divorce, the end of a relationship or a sudden death.

If you experienced one of these events, you might exhibit stress, anxiety, guilt, depression, anger or even confusion. In addition, you might have trouble sleeping, be continually tired, and have trouble concentrating. You may also feel tension within your body and more aches and pains.

To manage your symptoms, rely on positive self-management. You will find the tools to aid you in the following chapters. For example, deep breathing and body relaxation and reaching out to friends and your support system are encouraged. Be sure to engage in healthy exercise, eat well-balanced meals, avoid alcohol or drugs, and make positive use of your hobbies. Turn to your journal to aid in managing and venting your feelings. If you find that your emotions seem out of control, do not hesitate to obtain professional help through a qualified trauma expert.

The pandemic did not produce severe trauma for most of us, but an element of fear certainly swept the country. Why did people race to the store to stock up on toilet paper, soap, jugs of water, and other products to hold them if the pandemic lingered? Fear, combined with science, led people to don face masks, keep their distance, wipe counter tops, and wash their hands thoroughly.

The brain generated these fears and all the other emotions associated with COVID-19 and the COVID variants. Amazingly, we can process and concentrate, learn and recall, construct, invent, and create with such accuracy, much more effectively than any human-made computer recognizing the complexity of the brain. Yet, the brain only acts upon the information and data we feed it.

The brain believes what we tell it. It can believe fears, fantasies, dreams, lies, and love. If we believe that meth or heroin, alcohol, or chocolate makes us feel better physically or emotionally, the brain believes it and changes its chemistry to adapt to the need for the drug. The brain, armed with neurochemicals like dopamine, noradrenaline and serotonin, alters its receptor sites. Therefore, when we hear information, whether from a general conversation or a news broadcast, whether truth or lies, the brain adapts accordingly. If we read statistics or history, whether real or contrived, the brain again adapts. If we believe we are in love, the pleasure center activates, and the brain believes us.

Our reaction to COVID follows this pattern. If we reacted with fear, the brain altered its chemistry. If we fought the idea of the pandemic and ignored the warnings issued, the brain reacted. If we accepted the concept, the brain adapted to that as well. The brain adapts to all the information that we receive.

Now with COVID behind us or at least diffused or modified thanks to vaccinations, we can reprogram our brain to accept the new routines, even with the COVID variants. Yes, now you may be required to return to your office to work. You can no longer attend your meeting online only. And you must interact with staff and clients daily. But if you have adjusted well to working at home, you may feel frustrated at this change. However, since you have little choice, if you tell yourself that returning to work will give you a pleasant break from home and allow you to renew your acquaintance with co-workers, the brain will begin to accept the new information. If you continue to communicate the positive aspects of your new routine, the brain will come to believe the new message.

The good news is that the brain can be healed from any damage. Just as an addict can get clean and sober and can control cravings, we can alter our brain chemistry by changing our behaviors and thoughts. Yes, during the pandemic, the prevalence of fear and anxiety was undeniable. That's why, during these months, I have often suggested that patients turn off the TV, computer, or phone for a day or two. Let the brain rest. Pull your eyes away from the screen and give your ears a rest from the constant chatter. But just how do we do this? How do we find the road back after our brain has been so besieged?

I like to call this process **healing your mind**.

Step one in healing your mind is fairly simple. I compare it to yard work or gardening. If you have a beautiful green lawn or a bountiful flower garden, you must, of course, plant and water. However, if you do not pull the weeds, they will soon take over your lovely project. Weeds must go. You can pull by hand and sow some chemicals. How you choose to rid yourself of weeds is irrelevant. The important thing is to get rid of them.

Consider the mind and how it works. It will believe negative thoughts. Pull the weeds out before they grow. Later, in this book, I will list several exercises for removing negative thoughts. The key is to recognize them. Perhaps you are harboring ill will toward someone who holds different political views than you do. That's okay. They are entitled to their beliefs. Let it go. Perhaps your best friend refuses to wear a mask or distance himself. You disagree, but that doesn't need to destroy your friendship. You don't need to worry about the views of others. Take care of your garden.

Move your mind outside. Step outside into nature's grand landscape. Take a look around. Focus on one item. Perhaps that small bush that grows by the patio. Examine the leaves, the color, the texture, the branches, the twigs, and how it grows into the ground. Now, smell it deeply. Can you compare the smell to any substance you know? Listen. Does the bush move slightly in the wind and make a sound? What does it remind you of? Touch a leaf, then the branch. What does it feel like? Lick the leaf gently. Examine what the leaf tastes like for you.

This exercise is known as mindfulness, and I will refer to the process several times throughout this book because it is invaluable in calming stress and anxiety. It assists us in changing our thinking, our attitudes and our behaviors, essential to healing. I've included it here because I want you to begin to unlock your mind to nature and to the wonder of healing your mind when this unforeseen pandemic has assaulted it.

Nothing else will change until we begin shifting your mindset and you stop letting the chatter and the clatter distract you from renewing yourself. A key to successful renewal is unplugging your distracted thinking. Has your computer ever frozen on you? You keep watching that little circle on the screen that insists that it's thinking, downloading and upgrading new information. No matter how long you stare at it, it just keeps swirling around. At times it may pause long enough to display a blank screen, but the dang circle eventually pops back up. Try as you might, you can't get to your mail or photographs. In desperation, you unplug the device. You wait a few moments and plug it back in. Somehow, it has reset.

Your mind deserves to be unplugged. Not permanently unplugged, of course, but sometimes, and you need to unplug it only from the overpowering thoughts that are interrupting your journey to recovery. We all need quiet, peace, and restful sleep away from the entangled messages of the pandemic, which is when mindfulness can step in to provide the rest you need.

Sometimes that process might require reframing your mind or thinking process. Reframing includes identifying the elements of your thinking, including your life experiences and ideas, and how the mind references and responds to these things. By considering areas that create or contribute to problems in your life, you can then challenge yourself to make positive changes. Have you ever considered how negative thinking has stolen time and energy from you? When you allow yourself to focus on one point of view or one emotion, the brain absorbs that feeling. If you feed it a negative feeling or viewpoint, just like that weed in your garden, it can grow unchecked. At such times it's critical to examine your emotions surrounding the feeling and deliberately select the options, a different or more positive emotion or point of view.

A powerful example of reframing came from a young lady with cancer who appeared on *America's Got Talent* in June 2021. Jane Marczweski, whose stage name is Nightbirde, reported her survival odds were less than 2 percent. Upon completing her moving performance of her original song "It's Okay," she spoke with such positive confidence that I jotted her quote down. She said, "You can't wait until life isn't bad anymore to be happy."

To force yourself to look at feelings and self differently is not easy. It requires stopping the flurry of thoughts and shifting your mind to more positive thoughts. I'm sure this young woman must have had some mixed emotions initially, perhaps anxiety, anger, or even fear. But she has reprocessed her thinking into a meaningful message to inspire others to reach their goals.

Reframing may be especially difficult when it involves examining the people in your life. We all desire love, companionship and friendship. Sometimes in our quest, we allow others access to our innermost circle without reviewing their principles and values. While we may consider ourselves immune to negative influences, the reality is that without caution, we can end up making unwise choices that may have a profound effect on our lives.

Reframing and unplugging are essential as we readjust to life without the pandemic. It's easy to lose the mask, but when we step outside our house and face the barrage of humans, it can seem like aliens have invaded planet Earth while we were inside. If you are basically a shy, passive person, you can find yourself trembling at the notion and stumbling over words as you attempt conversation. If you are an extrovert, you may shudder at having to pull back since the variants surrounding COVID have emerged. Regardless of your personality style, don't panic. You may need to step back into the house now and then and unplug on the path to reframing your thoughts.

Reframing may mean further change. Have you ever had to weed someone out of your life? That person could be a close friend or even a family member. If so, you know how difficult this decision was. Did you try to compromise and allow them in selectively? You may have found this choice was even more confusing. The truth is that when people bring problems, trouble, chaos, and danger into our lives, we need to make some tough choices about our future. If you have experienced the sorrow of removing people from your life garden, you may also have recognized the peace that results.

Whether you use mindfulness, a form of unplugging, or reframing, recognize that this is *your* process. Shifting your mind is a challenge, and all persons must proceed at their own pace, often a small step at a time. Practice patience with yourself as you begin this process. Pick the actions you are ready to try, move at your own pace, and consult with others. You may have to regroup or recharge yourself and remove all the excess stimuli that the world now brings to your doorstep. Remember, the pandemic has challenged your brain. It will take time to recover. But you can launch your recovery by developing and practicing skills within the following chapters.

4

Launching Recovery

Shifting your mind or weeding your garden requires personal follow-up to bounce back from COVID and its variants successfully. Because the brain has experienced a form of trauma (yes, we have all been through trauma during the pandemic), it is important to review and do some self-analysis. What information and actions have impacted you during the pandemic? Are you recovering from COVID yourself or did your health seem to decline? Have you suffered a financial loss or the loss of social contact? Did you feel confused by seemingly inconsistent news reports?

You do not have to ignore or accept every piece of information you've heard or learned to get back to your reality. What is important is to accept that you've been through a huge trial, that all you've experienced has impacted you in some form. For some people, the impact may be less; for others, tremendous. But in the end, acknowledging the truth about yourself is what can bring lasting healing.

Finding the truth of yourself demands that you examine yourself objectively. This process can be overwhelming if you are honest about your successes and your shortcomings. I suggest you initially make a simple list of your preferences, of things you know about yourself. Try jotting your responses down in a notebook. This list might include some of the following items.

What is your favorite color?
Name your favorite actor or actress and why you like this person.
Describe your preferred music genre.
Specify your spiritual or religious journey.

Name your favorite family member and tell why that person is #1.

Explain your preferences—mornings or evenings?

Be creative and add other categories to draw a more inclusive picture of yourself. Continue with this self-review until you feel you have covered basic facts about yourself. At that point, you should expand your examination. Begin by recalling and writing down the various emotions you have experienced over the past week. Have you felt stressed at times? Angry that you have to go back to work in the office? Happy? Sad? Overwhelmed by all the breakfast cereal choices? Curious? Depressed? Excited? Tired? Bored? These emotions will vary from situation to situation, but the key is being honest with yourself as you jot your feelings down.

As you have been exploring the various feelings and truths, have you been writing them down? This process is often termed *journaling.* When you hear that term, is your first thought *I'm not a writer*? Journaling is not about being a writer but about sharing your emotions, all those pent-up frustrations about the Year of COVID. It's about relating your journey to your normal routines. There are no absolute rules about journaling. It is a ticket to reshaping your life. The journal is your private record to share or not to share—your choice.

Are you wondering how to begin your journal? Let's start with the words you've already written. Use a simple piece of paper or several pages bound together in a notebook. You do not need a fancy bound journal unless you want one. Or you could choose to write on a computer (hopefully, you will have a protected password or system). Add a pen or a pencil or a keyboard.

I suggest you jot down the date and time as you record your responses to the above items. Then you can write anything you like. One word or a dozen. A hundred if that's what you need. You are writing what you feel this day, this time. It could be as simple as "COVID sucks!" or "Damn him anyway!" or "They are all lying." Maybe that's all you want to write for now. Just a few simple words to vent your emotions. Later, you may want to detail entire incidents. How did the situation make you feel? That's the key point. Write and journal your feelings. Vent. Start small and work up to more frequent and perhaps even daily journaling.

The content can be positive. Describe the beautiful morning sunset, the purple bird of an unknown species you witnessed on your neighbor's fence. The new puppy and his attempts to walk. Describe happiness, peaceful moments, contented times, disappointment, grief, anger, guilt—all of the human emotions we all have. There is no specific process for your journey.

What is the purpose of journaling? First of all, you are venting some strong feelings, getting them out, and, in the process, working them out in your mind. We are all like pressure cookers. The steam builds inside us and, if we don't vent, don't slowly release the valve, we can burst. By journaling, you are exploring yourself and how you feel about events and people in your life. You are evaluating whether your point of view is accurate or the only one. You are prioritizing your problems and setting some goals. All of this, of course, takes place over time.

Time is a true friend of journaling. What you write today you should read again in two weeks, a month, three months. Again, no absolute rule on this. But it is important to reread what you've written to determine if you are making any progress in your thinking and if you are moving your mind in a direction away from the pandemic. Journaling helps you expand accountability for your past actions and sets the groundwork for possible changes in your attitude. This change is especially critical if you are working on addiction problems. Journaling can help you examine triggers that have led you to use drugs or engage in other addictive behaviors.

Journaling helps you to examine yourself in simple ways. Here are some sample questions.

- What are three things I am grateful for?
- What do I miss from high school?
- What is my favorite color, and why?
- Who was my first romance?
- What is my lifetime goal ?
- What are three reasons I got a divorce?
- If I could choose a different career, what would it be?

This list could go on indefinitely. You can create your list as you use your journal as an excellent means of self-reflection. This reflection can include using your personal spiritual and religious resources and inspirations. Perhaps meditation and other moments of quiet reflection can follow your daily journaling to aid you in accepting all the complexities of who you are.

Don't forget to examine your feelings throughout the entire period of the pandemic. What were your initial feelings? How about as the days and weeks passed? Did your moods vary considerably depending upon the situation? Describe these feelings. Did you feel like you needed medication or therapy at times? List both positive and negative emotions you have felt, which is a substantial step in reaching objective self-awareness.

Another simple method of finding your truth is to make a grocery list. My grocery list will not be like yours. I start at the front of the store and jot down the items as they occur on my usual journey. You may shop differently. But the important thing is to note the key items needed for completing your weekly meal plans. If you are planning a Thanksgiving dinner, the turkey may be at the top of the list, followed by yams, pumpkin pie, and whipped cream. If you think of your personal needs this way, it can help you jot down your truths. What is at the top of your list? What has impacted your life the most over the past months?

Your list—call it brainstorming, if you like—can be as long or as disorganized as you like. But the important thing is to list the various items that impacted you. You can be as specific as you like. Did it enrage you the way someone responded to an item you posted on Facebook? Did you get into a physical or verbal altercation over what someone said or did to you? Were you unable to contain your rage? Did you go on a binge? Perhaps you were infuriated because, during the early days of the pandemic, those hoarders bought all the toilet paper in your store, and you were left with only six rolls in your house. If you tend to enjoy the solitude of your home, you still prefer not to leave, even after all the masks have come off and you've been fully vaccinated.

Hopefully, you found a dozen pleasant moments during the pandemic. Maybe your children called to say, "Are you okay? We love you." You binged your favorite TV show. Perhaps you learned to cook a new meal or read a book you'd wanted to read for several years. Maybe it just felt peaceful to be by yourself for a few weeks.

Sometimes it takes more than journaling and self-analysis.

Reach out to friends for support, those willing to make truthful comments to aid in your quest. Some words of warning, though: friends may hesitate to hurt your feelings; they may make remarks that do hurt your feelings, you fail to see their words as positive criticism, and the friendship suffers; they may be too overburdened by their problems to listen, and you feel snubbed.

An outside source, such as a counselor or therapist, can provide a more objective view and offer suggestions for healthy change. This support person can also guide you in the process of reframing and other cognitive behavior tools. If needed, they can also provide and monitor personality and other tests, which can guide the development of your progress.

Following acceptance of yourself and how you managed during COVID, the next step is a process known as *forgiveness,* which may sound a bit strange. You did not cause COVID. You are not responsible for what others or governments did or didn't do. You managed to get through this pandemic mostly unscathed—at least physically. The after-effects may seem more overwhelming for you. This type of forgiveness has more to do with our personal negative and destructive thoughts—not just with COVID. For example, past actions, such as neglecting your children or committing a crime, can create a sense of guilt. The use of drugs and alcohol might create a lingering sense of shame. In such cases, forgiving yourself and accepting yourself is critical to moving forward.

The concept of acceptance is familiar to Alcoholics Anonymous (AA), which uses the Twelve Step program to lead to sobriety. The steps include the importance of having a higher power to help participants remove character defects and other shortcomings. Your focus on continual improvement is emphasized as an ongoing quest. Someone once said, "Wise people continue to improve throughout their lives. Others fail to progress."

Would you like a jump start to bounce back from COVID? As you read through this book, you will find many skills, exercises, and suggestions. However, a very effective way to begin the process is through *visualization.* What exactly is meant by visualization? You may think of it as imagining an event, fantasizing, recalling, planning, or a waste of time. It may encompass all of the above. But visualization, as used in a therapeutic sense, includes many other facets.

Visualization is a method of gaining control over your thoughts, of employing new methods or skills to aid you in managing your emotions and reactions to events—even the confusion surrounding COVID.

A dictionary definition might read "visualization is the formation of a mental image of something or the representation of an object, situation, or a set of information or other images." It is sometimes confused with meditation. But in meditation, the mind concentrates while the body relaxes, which is also one way to begin visualization. Visualization is one method of using the mind to influence the body. Both techniques have the power to teach and heal.

Visualization techniques can provide motivation, remind you of your goals, and inspire you to keep working to achieve your goals. It can instill confidence, offer you a chance to relive past and rehearse future scenarios, and aid you in reducing stress. Reducing stress is a very important advantage while the pandemic continues to impact us. Just when we thought we could remove our masks, variants arose to destabilize our thoughts further.

Visualization is directly connected to mindfulness or the quality or state of being aware or conscious of something. *Mindfulness*, referred to frequently in this book, is a mental state in which you focus on the present moment but acknowledge and accept feelings and thoughts and body sensations. These concepts are a part of visualization, with exceptions in which you deliberately and with purpose remove your thoughts from the present to achieve a healthy goal.

One method of managing the fallout from tragic events, from personal failures and "wish I would haves," is to envision them differently or think of them in a different context. If you consider the variety of responses to COVID-19 and the variants that can further impact your thinking, you can discover new ways of managing your emotions—vital to bouncing back.

Visualization provides a key method of restoring calm, peace, and harmony to your life. Visualization rejuvenates the brain and restores the nerves and joints in your body. It reactivates your sense of the wonder and joy in nature and humanity. By combining the concepts of brainstorming, mindfulness, and reframing, you will be well on your way toward self-managing any personal or exterior conflicts.

But don't forget to journal your responses to the following ideas and exercises of visualization!

Sometimes, you may wish to take out crayons and draw a picture of what you are feeling. Observe the colors you choose.

Let's examine several visualization exercises to aid as you manage the ups and downs of life, whether they be personal difficulties or any widespread crises, such as COVID.

Filing cabinets: We all need boundaries in our life. Have you ever felt overwhelmed by the many things you are required to do—at work, at home, maintaining your health, family responsibilities? If you don't break these activities down into doable items, you may be tempted to throw up your hands and say, "What the hell! I can't do this anymore!" We all need file cabinets in our life.

To activate your filing cabinets, do a mindful exercise. Start with sitting down, placing your feet on the floor, taking deep belly breaths, then relaxing and closing your eyes. Now allow yourself to visualize a room with filing cabinets to the right and left and in front of you. The drawers are all open. Label them. Work. Kids. Yard. Health. Bills. Whatever is on your mind. One at a time, close the drawers. This does not mean that you will never manage the closed cabinets. But for this hour, or day or week, close them. Keep open the *one* that you must manage right now—your priority.

Practice this skill daily. Close your cabinets daily or even hourly, if needed. Keep focused on the one thing necessary at this time. This process enriches your sense of boundaries. I don't need to worry about my son's problems with his girlfriend. I don't need to worry about the new masking rules in my favorite restaurant.

Armor: Putting on your suit of armor is another method to aid you in setting boundaries and protecting yourself from hurtful words and events and confusion. Harmful words and events can strike your armor, but they don't pierce it. They bounce off. Sure, they might hurt. Maybe they slightly wound you, but they don't kill you. Again, visualize yourself with that armor when someone verbally assaults you. The bullets bounce off, and you have time to recover, to manage the attack healthily.

Clouds and balloons: Do you ever experience angry thoughts? Of course you do. You are human. Some things, like COVID, for example, can make us angry. People can push our buttons. How do you manage when you have an angry, depressed or anxious thought? One answer is in clouds and balloons. Examine the cartoon panels in your local newspaper. Note that the characters' thoughts and conversations are depicted in balloons above their heads. You can do the same.

You just learned that you can no longer dine inside your favorite restaurant; you might be very angry. You might say something like "I thought this COVID thing was over. Now, a new kind of COVID is screwing everything up again. I'm so mad. I'm even depressed." When you encounter other negative situations and thoughts, a simple exercise is to allow yourself to experience that feeling for a few moments, but then visualize the words as black clouds or balloons floating over your head.

If you are in a relaxed position, that is an added aid. Now lift your arm gently and easily and slowly push one of the dark clouds to one side. Then another. You can replace it with a smiley face if you like. You can also talk to the dark cloud in your head or out loud. Say something simple like "Go away for the next two hours. Then we'll discuss it for five minutes. Then we're done for today."

Practice pushing dark balloons away two or three times per day and replace them with yellow and red balloons, bright ones with happy faces, which can get to be a refreshing and pleasant activity.

Fantasies: Sometimes, we think that daydreaming and fantasizing are a sign that we are not mentally sound, but this usually is not true. Fantasy is the foundation of the arts—painting, drawing, writing, creating music, making movies, devising electronics. The list is endless. Steve Jobs meditated, and the iPhone was the result. Where would we be without the imagination of Einstein, Tesla, Marconi, Rembrandt, Shakespeare, the Beatles? Imagination and fantasy are critical to creation.

How does this apply to your mental health and managing the emotions in your life? Some fantasies can be dark. For example, imagining harming another person or obsessing over past personal or historic events to avoid pleasant and present activities. These types of fantasies may need to be swept away with the dark clouds or more intense therapy.

The upside of fantasy is that it is entertaining, providing access to healing and goal setting. Entertaining can include creating stories or pleasant thoughts in your mind. You might enjoy having a romance with your favorite film star or singer. Weaving a tale to occupy a boring afternoon may provide an outlet for your sensual emotions. As long as your behavior is not obsessive or does not detract from your goals or real-life duties, no harm done.

Healing includes using fantasy to relive incidents, especially trauma-instilled incidents, so it is often best performed in specialized therapy. One method involves visualizing yourself as a small child living with emotional pain brought about by neglect or physical or sexual abuse. This child has no one to help or save him. You can visualize yourself as the adult in your mind and step in to comfort the child. You can't save the child, but you can comfort and reassure him that you are there for support.

Another type of visualization that can provide healing is the empty chair. In this activity, you select a person with whom you have an unresolved conflict or a negative emotional history. They are not present or may be deceased. Imagine them being in the chair, which is your opportunity to explain your pain to them and let them know how their actions or failure affected you. Because this type of work can result in strong emotional reactions, it is recommended that another trusting support person, preferable a counselor or a therapist, be present.

Finally, fantasizing offers the opportunity for goal setting. Imagine yourself as successful, sitting in an office or operating on a patient. Seeing yourself wheeling your grocery cart past the potato chip aisle and your scales showing a two-pound loss is another example. Several other types of visualization offer further methods to address reaching goals.

Poster board and sticky notes: Another visualization process requires materials such as a poster board and sticky notes, but you can visualize the poster board and sticky notes in your mind. Perhaps your goal is to obtain a master's degree in criminal justice. To do so, you must take several steps. Jot those steps down on the sticky notes and place them on the poster board, which can be perceived much like the boards depicted on television crime shows, where the characters draw lines and pin photos and move things about, trying to reach conclusions. What comes first? How much education? How much training? What is the cost? Can you fill out applications for scholarships? Place your goal at the end and visualize yourself holding your diploma. Keep your poster board in a visible area and look at it several times a week; read the notes. Move them around as you complete one goal or one is altered.

Crystal ball or magic wand: None of us can see into the future. But if you could, what would you like to happen? These tools can be used to help with setting goals. Visualize a crystal ball and stare into it. Where would you like to see yourself in five years, ten years? Place yourself at that desk, behind that camera, accepting that award, getting that big check, whatever your goal is. Write down your goal on a piece of paper and place it on your refrigerator. Read it each time you open the door. You can imagine that crystal ball at various times throughout the day and see yourself meeting your goals.

You can also visualize a magic wand that removes your obstacles. What are the hurdles you have to overcome to reach your goals? Is COVID and its variants standing in your way right now? Touch them with your wand. They will not be here forever. Finances? Can you get a scholarship, borrow funds, take a second job? Visualize the wand. Does this process make all the obstacles disappear? Of course not. But it does provide incentive and hope and encouragement that you can find a way to reach your goals.

These skills are but a start toward finding and enjoying contentment and harmony in your life. I urge you to try those that work for you. Reach out to a counselor or a therapist for the most complex exercises. Future chapters will provide many other valuable skills to use on your journey of self-reflection. One of those is covered in the next chapter, as we discuss the importance of medical and mental health on your path to revitalizing yourself after COVID.

5

A Healthier You

Has your car been sitting for weeks with limited use? It may need an oil change or a new fuel filter. We are no different. We need a comprehensive check-up after months of ignoring the aches and pains of our bodies. You may have attributed your headaches and stiff joints to stress and swallowed a couple of aspirin. Or you may have panicked at times, wondering if your symptoms indicated COVID. Did your fear keep you from an annual examination, or did you miss an appointment with a specialist? Did you ignore an aching tooth? And how about that stress? If the answer to the above questions is "yes," you may now be wondering how to approach renewing your body and spirit.

You may be one of the fortunate folks who managed to exercise, walk in the park, or otherwise burn energy. Perhaps you were able to monitor your caloric intake. Perhaps you have a wide range of activities that keep you occupied, physically and emotionally. If so, you have a head start on reshaping yourself after the pandemic.

But many of you experienced limitations in caring for your bodies and minds during the months of disruption and uncertainty. Getting back to regaining your stability and maintaining health will require a full medical check-up, a dental exam, and a mental health review. The second part of this chapter will provide some guidelines to aid you in that process.

For now, let's take a look at activities that can help restore the energy and vitality that you enjoyed before the COVID-19 intrusion. As you review the suggestions for reactivating yourself, please use those that work for you. Take a look at how nutrition, activity, sleep, proper use of medication, and goal setting can positively impact your revitalization.

Nutrition

I hate the word diet. I think most of us do. It implies doing without, restriction and living on kale and carrots. But proper nutrition is not a diet. It is not suffering and feeling guilty when you have that scoop of ice cream. It is not cooking with exotic ingredients and buying expensive meals delivered by mail.

Proper nutrition means evaluating your body's needs. Ask yourself, "What is food, anyway?" It is a fuel source. Food provides energy to our bodies, so we desire it to engage in activities. It is brain food, enabling us to process and think. It contributes to improved sleep cycles.

Furthermore, a board-certified physician, Dr. Irvin Cohen, emphasizes the importance of proper diet and good health as an aid to building and maintaining our immune system during COVID-19. His book *Fighting COVID-19, the Unequal Opportunity Killer* is a must-read for those with chronic medical problems such as diabetes. Dr. Cohen also points out that the type of foods we eat can drive hunger and cravings, causing us to eat even more. Before undertaking any diet or nutrition program, consult with your medical provider.

By eating wisely and determining what works for you, you can also instill calmness in your mind, pushing away much of the stress, anxiety, and depression brought about by the pandemic. Yes, during the pandemic, many people found their eating habits disrupted. If you felt content spending most of your time at home, did you get sidetracked or sloppy with meal preparation? Did you skip meals? Did you overeat? Examining personal patterns is important to determine if you can benefit from making healthy changes to your meal plans. Are you consciously incorporating vegetables, fruits, grains and nuts into your diet? Trying to get enough of the right fiber and protein and plant material can be a challenge.

Much of healthy eating is about choices. Grocery shopping can be a downfall for many of us. So many temptations. It's easy to grab a bag of chips, a package of cookies, or some donuts for breakfast, and let's not forget the candy bar at the checkout stand. Choices are not confined to the grocery store. With COVID, we were somewhat limited in eating out, except when takeout was available. It was so easy to grab a burger, fries and soda. But with the departure of the pandemic, the choices may seem unlimited, almost overwhelming. Now you must walk the aisles and make selections that may appear new and even frightening when you've been confined for so long.

Many of us like quick and easy meals, frozen and microwaveable, so we make impulsive decisions that often are not in our best interests. Some experts consider this a reason why Americans rank among the most overweight people in the world. In addition, we often rationalize that we don't have time to prepare "proper" meals or that the ingredients are often more expensive than cheaper, carbohydrate-heavy meals.

When we have prepared meals at home during the pandemic, we may have made starchy dishes like pasta, and we have made our own bread. Some of us grew up on those meals—potatoes and beans, maybe corn as a side dish. Our grandparents, who labored on farms or worked long, physical hours in factories, burned off these calories. Historically, many areas of our country did not have access to seasonal fruits and vegetables.

The world is different now, and we do have more access. Today, even in restricted areas, we can obtain fresh lettuce, cabbage, pears, apples, berries, and nuts. Often it is just a matter of planning—making those healthy food choices through planning and budgeting to enjoy satisfying meals.

For those who struggle with weight, the first step is to consult with your medical provider. If you have a serious medical condition, such as diabetes, you will want to make food choices that keep you safe and healthy. Avoiding certain products and watching your sugar intake may be critical to your ongoing health. This information is not a substitute for consulting with your doctor or nutritionist. Many medical teams include certified nutritionists. Make use of the education and guidance available from such experts.

Is weight management just a matter of avoiding all the "bad" foods? No, again, it is a matter of choices. If you struggle with cutting back on your consumption, try switching to a smaller plate or placing fewer items on your plate. Even better, cook less food. You may have noticed that many restaurants serve oversized portions. Some people choose to share the meal with a partner or friend.

To begin your journey to healthier choices, make a list. Use your journal to write down everything you eat in one normal week. Don't cheat. List everything, even the three crackers and one cookie you grabbed as you passed through the kitchen. Now consider which items you can easily eliminate. The next time you visit the store, be tough on yourself. You don't need the cookies. This process of slowly cutting back can be compared to breaking an alcohol or drug addiction. Realize that you are not going to be successful all the time, but you are growing through this process. Do reward yourself with a healthy snack.

What about scales? Some experts say avoid weighing often, whether you are struggling to lose weight or gain weight. There is no rigid rule about this. But you do need to weigh at least once a week to see if you are meeting your goals and making progress. Experts often recommend a weight loss of no more than two to four pounds a month. Do not let the scales become a dictator. Do not let the numbers make you feel guilty or like you are a failure. Stick with the program recommended by your physician and nutritionist.

Avoid rigid and fad diets. There are many productive and healthy diet plans out there. Look them over but realize that many plans want you to buy their product, book, or food. They may be very useful as long as they contain nutritious meals, and if you have the funds, you may want to incorporate them into your meal planning.

Eat breakfast! If that sounds obvious, it should be. However, many people who struggle with being overweight or underweight often skip breakfast. Starting with a full tank of gas revs up your vehicle. Follow with lunch and dinner, but, as noted previously, watch the portions. Also, don't forget to snack in between, avoiding potato chips and cookies. Focus on healthy snacks. Select the apple, maybe a celery stick with peanut butter, perhaps some nuts.

Don't forget to hydrate. Water is essential to the healthy functioning of our body and mind. Water assists our blood system by supplying oxygen and nutrients to our cells. It helps our kidneys to get rid of waste. It also lubricates our joints and eyes, helps with our digestive system, and keeps our skin healthy. Low levels of water can result in headaches, dizziness, lethargy, and poor concentration. Over the long term, dehydration can cause urinary tract infections, constipation, and kidney stones.

Adults need to drink about eight to ten glasses of water per day. Fluid intake also depends upon your physical activity and the weather. Almost all liquid drinks can count toward promoting hydration, including milk, tea, coffee, and juice. However, the consensus is that the best form is plain water. In addition, fruits and vegetables contribute valuable fluids.

Begin thinking of water and food as your body's fuel for a healthier you. Reframe your thinking from "I want" or "I need" or "I love." Instead, say aloud, "My body is empty," "I need energy today," "I feel hungry," "I feel thirsty." Repeat these messages to yourself several times before meals, and you may find they help you examine why you consume certain foods.

The reality is that we don't usually think about our food as we shovel our meals and snacks into our mouths, which sounds rather harsh but is true. Whether it's a cracker or a cucumber, we don't stop and consider how the item affects our sense of enjoyment and pleasure. To better understand this concept, you might use *mindful eating* to explore your reactions to the foods you most enjoy. Mindful eating is one type of mindfulness, a way to use your senses to enjoy your food in a grateful and relaxed way.

To implement this process, begin by selecting a product, any healthy food product. For this exercise, let's use an apple. Upon completing your exercise, to get the full experience, journal your responses.

Now, take a few moments to savor each of the following steps.

1. View the apple. Examine it closely. What color is it? What shape is it? Does it have a stem? Does it have any blemishes? Is it pleasing to the eye?
2. Pick the apple up and rub your fingers against the skin. What does it feel like? Is it smooth? Feel the stem. What emotion do you feel when you touch it?
3. Smell the apple, take a deep breath. Describe the scent. Does it evoke any special memories?
4. Hold it up to your ear. Does it make a sound? No? Can you imagine what it would sound like if it had a sound?
5. Bite into the apple. Roll the bite around in your mouth, savor it. Hold it. Now, chew it. Roll it around again and swallow. How does it feel as it slides down your throat?

As you complete this exercise, take a few moments and review your responses to the questions. Make a note of your feelings and sensations in your journal. You don't need to do this process for every bite you eat, but the idea is to take your time as you consume your food. Enjoy it. Recognize it for the value it brings to your well-being. Reflect on your gratitude for the gift of food. And, yes, now and then, repeat this mindful eating exercise to remind yourself of the need to appreciate the sensory world around you.

As you recharge and refuel, you may feel the urge for more activity. Engaging in overeating or skipping meals in the past stifled your energy and enabled sluggish chemicals to infect your brain. Your body now craves and demands more activity. As you add high-octane fuel to your system, your engine runs smoother. You can select those activities that lead to a healthier and happier you.

Activity

Movement is essential to our well-being. But how much movement did you get during COVID? Perhaps you were sent home from work one day, thinking you would return within a week or two, but it never happened. Working from home, you found yourself sucked into a laid-back daily lifestyle. Most of us did not move in the same manner as we did before this pandemic. Many people confined themselves to the couch, watching too much TV or playing too many games. Did you find yourself succumbing to the comfort of this inactivity? Perhaps you were among those who walked, jogged, ran, or worked out. Even if you walked on occasion, did you limit the energy and time you devoted to exercise?

Reviewing your physical activity is essential before beginning any exercise program. Remember, you do not have to engage in rigid workouts. The key to maintaining health is activity, and there are many types of activity. One exercise you can do anywhere is simply walking in place, holding onto the back of a chair. Another exercise is to move your feet back and forth or your knees up and down while sitting in a chair. Rotate your arms and stretch your fingers. Doing the dishes, laundry, and other household chores also provides some exercise, as does working in the yard. These are all valuable activities for keeping your organs functioning well and keeping your brain active.

If you have been routinely engaged in more vigorous activities, please continue and do even more, if reasonable. If you have access to a gym and use the machines, more power to you. If you run relays and swim, wonderful. Keep up your routine. Consider setting your alarm clock for a time to work out each day regardless of the level of activity, making the ten- or fifteen-minute break part of your routine.

Perhaps you are unable physically or mentally to engage in high-energy exercises. If you are disabled and have medical restrictions, you will want to do those activities that are safe for you. You should consult your physician before attempting any that are not advised. Some of you may increase your activity level but will need to work up to a healthy level. Again, consult with your medical provider before engaging in any difficult or strenuous exercise that you haven't attempted before.

You may be the person seeking a new activity, one that will generate excitement and rejuvenation after living in the COVID world for so many months. Warning: if you have been content in your cottage, doing word games, and restricting contact with other people, it may be difficult, even fearful at times, to engage in more open activities. But be patient with yourself. Examine the following list, and you may find something that works for you and that you can ease into more comfortably. All of the following activities are also diversions. In other words, when you are feeling anxious or depressed, engaging in any one can pull your thoughts from that negative emotion to a more mindful moment.

Ride a bike: This exercise promotes strength, balance, and a breath of fresh air. Of course, certain disabled individuals may not be able to engage in this activity, but for those who can do so, it offers a way to contemplate nature and wave at your neighbors.

Start a garden: This activity offers an opportunity to examine the soil beneath your feet, seeds, and water—the very elements of life. Watching your flowers or vegetables as they sprout can make you feel a sense of awe and gratitude for the wonders of nature. For those living in apartments, consider rooftop or windowsill gardens.

Go for a walk: Much like riding a bike, walking provides exercise and involves setting a goal, perhaps going around one block one time, two the next time, perhaps a mile in time. Walking can be done with a friend, a group or alone.

Read a book: This activity removes your mind from your present environment, including anxiety and stress, acting as a pleasant diversion. You can be engaged in a mystery, a fantasy or a romance.

Bake cookies: This fun activity can involve other family members. You can experiment with new recipes or make up some interesting combinations. Cookies baking adds a pleasant and uplifting aroma to your home and buoys your spirit.

Learn to play a musical instrument: Learning something new generates brain activity and provides you with a positive feeling of accomplishment.

Dance: Dance offers the extra benefit of enjoying music. Turn on the music, embrace the sounds, and find the rhythm. Now, allow your body to freestyle to the beat. Dance, like many exercises, burns calories. Don't forget to do an impromptu dance to incidental music on radio and TV when the spirit moves you.

Play sports: Select a sport that is appropriate for your physical condition. It could be softball, volleyball, golf, or just playing hoops in your backyard. Again, find an activity that you enjoy and that brings enthusiasm and pleasure to your day.

Paint your bedroom: Wow, this sounds like work. But it can be fun. You can pick a color or design, maybe follow up with a new bedspread and pillows. You might be able to enlist the help of family and friends. This activity should keep your thoughts occupied as you see the progress and experience a sense of beauty and satisfaction.

Build a birdhouse: Constructing an object, whether from wood, foam board, or plastic, provides a sense of achievement. Whether you follow a self-designed plan or use a kit, the result can be the same. When you mount the birdhouse in your backyard or place it outside a window, you have only to glance at it to relive the process and experience the joy of completion.

Pull weeds: Oh, that sounds like a lot of work. Yes, but work that can burn energy and help get rid of stress and anxiety. Once more, you have expended calories while engaging in some much-needed yard work.

Of all the activities mentioned above, one activity generally ranks above all others—walking. If you are physically able, walk.

Once I met a man who weighed almost 500 pounds. He had diabetes and took insulin. The last time I spoke with him, he weighed half that and controlled his diabetes with diet only. I asked him how he had accomplished this. He said, "I walk. I walk every day. Even when it hurts, I walk." Now I don't recommend you walk until you hurt. But with your medical provider, you can establish a suitable and healthy walking regime.

Walking has added benefits. When the weather is mild, and spring arrives, opening buds and producing bee and bird sounds, we have the joy of experiencing nature. Take the earbuds out and listen, let your eyes scan the trees, the grass, the beauty of the clouds above. Breathe. Your mind is opening to the wonders around you and producing those awesome brain chemicals, serotonin, dopamine, and noradrenaline. You are renewing yourself, and guess what? This just might help with those sleepless nights.

Sleep

As the pandemic raged on, did you sleep too much? Did you suffer from sleep disturbances, up and down all night? Were you unable to turn your thoughts off no matter what you tried? Did you find yourself tired all day, unable to function? Perhaps you already had sleep problems, and the pandemic made them worse. If you experienced one or more of these responses, you are not alone.

Many people found themselves struggling with sleep issues. Some may have sought to get regular sleep through over-the-counter medications. Others may have called a therapist or obtained prescription medications. But most people simply endured, telling themselves that it would get better after COVID.

Sleep disturbances are fairly common today. We have much competition for our attention while our ancestors went to bed when it got dark. Oh, they may have lit a candle or used a lantern to check the livestock. But, on the whole, life rotated around the rising and setting of the sun. Then, along came those geniuses like Nikola Tesla, who invented alternating current, so we now have twenty-four-hour electricity in our homes. Of course, we are grateful for this marvelous invention. However, it also means that we can sit up all night watching TV, reading our favorite books, doing household chores, or hosting parties.

That's what we do. Many people now extend their waking hours into the evening by staring at the TV and binging their favorite series. Some stare into their cell phones, where they can also watch movies, see clips of concerts, play games, or scan their email or Facebook pages. Others play games singly and interactively on their game devices. Staring into the screens is more than just delaying bedtime. The screens activate certain chemicals in our brains. When we turn off the device, the senses do not just immediately shut down. Instead, they continue to stimulate our nervous system, interfering with the "shut down" period.

These devices also can interfere with an established routine. Routine is essential to our well-being as humans, just as sunrise and sunset marked the confines of day in the past. Routine provides security, a sense that we know what comes next. When we disrupt or juggle the normal routine in our lives, the natural sleep cycle is distorted.

The body goes through a series of sleep stages each night. These stages allow us to recuperate. Both the body and the brain require rest if we are to function effectively. When we do not experience healthy sleep, the fallout can be substantial, affecting our ability to reason, think, and remember. We can also experience fluctuations in our emotions, such as feeling grouchy, irritable, depressed, or stressed. We may feel tired, achy, unable to navigate our daily routines.

Several factors besides electronic distractions interfere with our sleep patterns. Some people have medical problems, such as sleep apnea, narcolepsy, frequent urination, or other serious conditions that should be addressed with their medical provider. Other behaviors that should best be addressed with your doctor include falling asleep during the day, frequent mood changes, or excessive snoring at night. Keep in mind that the use of alcohol or caffeine can also disrupt a person's sleep pattern.

The pandemic, of course, did nothing to contribute to sound sleep patterns. Perhaps you spent sleepless nights wondering if your mother's coughs and fever were COVID. Were you overwhelmed by the constant wiping of counters and doorknobs or trying to keep your hands from touching your face? When your head finally hit the pillow, you were so ready to sleep. But it didn't come. You tossed and turned. Maybe you got back up after an hour and fetched a brownie.

But that's all behind you. You should be able to relax now, and at times enjoy your life minus a mask. Still, you struggle with the sleep ogre. So, what can you do? How can you re-establish a healthy sleep routine, one that will result in your waking rested and ready for a productive day?

Perhaps it is time for you to reevaluate your sleep routine. One effective way to do so is by keeping a sleep diary or opening up your journal once more. Start at the beginning of the day, when you first rise and eat breakfast. If you are feeling tired and sleepy, make a note of that. During the day, if you find your eyes closing, your head nodding, stop and jot it down. You probably can't carry the diary around all day and write down every movement or feeling but do note anything of significance.

As the evening begins and the day winds down, make no changes in your usual routine, but write down times and actions. The important part of the journal may occur about mid-afternoon, when you begin to feel run-down, irritable, and achy. Jot down those symptoms. Continue to chart this for three or four days. Now, sit down and critically review your patterns. Are some actions preventing you from getting a good night's sleep?

You may find that many of your sleep problems lie within the failure to manage your routine healthily. Let's examine several areas that might improve your sleep patterns.

Keep a regular bedtime, even on weekends. You've worked all week. You're tired, but you stay up and binge a favorite series on Friday night. Heck, you can sleep in the next morning. Avoid this. Of course, there can be exceptions like birthdays and holidays. But, overall, resist the temptation. Your brain will appreciate your thoughtfulness. If you work a night schedule, reverse your sleep pattern, but stick to it once established.

Allow yourself an hour or two to wind down after a busy day. Our brain does not just shut down when we hop into bed. The distractions of the day remain with us. The "undone" items circle around us; guilt raises its head for all the missed calls, the forgotten appointment or the unresolved fight with your boss. Make a concerted effort to separate your work life from your personal life. Your spouse and kids will appreciate you for that. This process, known as *boundary setting*, has the added benefit of keeping work frustrations in their place, so you don't take them out on the family. It also works in reverse so that home stressors don't spill over into the workplace.

Avoid caffeinated drinks and alcoholic beverages during the last two hours before you go to bed. Caffeine and alcohol activate brain chemicals that interfere with the "shut down." Caffeine is a stimulant which is why many of us race for the coffee machine first thing in the morning—to get us going. Alcohol, on the other hand, is a depressant, and its use often stimulates greater consumption, especially in those with an alcohol problem, and it has been said to affect every organ in the body. In addition, the use of alcohol can cause tempers to flare and lead to disagreements and elevated brain chemicals, thus interfering with the sleep process.

Avoid food those last two hours. Eating near bedtime also produces a "full feeling," even leading to digestive sounds and aches and uncomfortable feelings while you are trying to drift off.

Turn off the electronic devices. Do not use while in bed. This was reviewed earlier but bears repeating. That screen glare can dive into your brain. But it's not just that. It's the last email you read, that interesting video, the Facebook post that caught your attention. All of that is still in your brain, circulating around and vying for your interest.

Turn off the lights. Night is the natural time when our world rests. Well, for most of nature, maybe not owls. But we are not owls, and most research indicates that we move into that initial sleep stage when we turn out the bright, glaring lights. The light, again, stimulates the brain and says, "Get up and read your book or play a game." Be firm with Mr. Light Bulb. Tell him, "Go away," and flip the switch.

Use earplugs or other means to block noise. If you live with other people, you have probably discovered they keep a different schedule than you do. Maybe your spouse works the night shift and sleeps during the day. You may need to sleep in another room and close the door. Request they turn the TV down or use their earphones to listen to their programs while you get some shut eye. Or get your own earplugs. Sound also filters through the air vents. You may be able to close them.

Make sure your bedding is comfortable. Sometimes, we don't even consider the effect of our bed and bedding on our ability to sleep soundly. Most of us can't afford to run out and purchase a new bed. However, we can get new sheets, blankets, and pillows. Bedding is primarily used to keep us warm in the winter and keeps our thermostats down. The pillow often is a culprit in poor sleep, as we fold it, twist it, and hug it.

You may want to decide if you need a fan for the summer heat or a small heater to keep the winter chill at bay. Some people also benefit from a white noise machine, which blocks outside noises and provides a relaxing sound to help with sleep induction.

After reviewing this list, begin to eliminate items that detract from healthy sleep patterns. Continue with journaling your activities. Note any improvement in your sleep patterns. A word of warning: do not give up on yourself if you still struggle with sleep at times. You may need to review and modify items to fit your needs. For example, if you work at night and sleep during the day, you may need blackout curtains in your bedroom.

Once more, do not hesitate to consult with your medical doctor as needed. Past trauma and mental health problems can contribute significantly to sleep loss. In addition, you may benefit from visiting with a therapist to aid you in managing anxiety and depression that are creating distractions. After consulting with these professionals, you may find that you can benefit from prescribed medication to aid your sleep as you continue to reshape yourself.

Medication

Stress, depression, and other human conditions did not just automatically go away when the pandemic passed. You may have issued a huge sigh of relief that you no longer were required to wear masks to your grocery store or distance yourself from loved ones. However, for many, these limits are still in place and the long months of being restricted may have created fallout symptoms that simply do not vanish.

Trying to acclimate to life after COVID may seem difficult for you. Increasing your social interaction and contact with co-workers means that you are now subject to a barrage of noise. Exposure to increased noise at various volumes can produce increased anxiety and even depressive symptoms, depending upon the types of triggers generated. Music, explosions, airplanes, traffic, or people talking can be a threat to your hearing or even damage your health. You may have felt relieved when COVID variants arose, suggesting further isolation.

Adjusting to the sounds of loud groups of people all cheering for their favorite baseball team or the mall music non-stop can play a role in your reactions or responses. How so? This noise stimulates the amygdala, which regulates the stress response. In turn, this can raise blood pressure and levels of cortisol, a stress-related hormone. In addition, this chronic stress is known to affect our immune system and contribute to serious medical problems and mental health illnesses.

Thus, even with the passing of the pandemic, many people may find that the adjustment will require more than just changing their diet, activity, and thinking process. Some people may benefit from psychotropic medications to help with the transition.

Perhaps you had never taken any medication before COVID, but you found your emotions were high and low, up and down during that time. As a result, you contacted your doctor and began a medication regime that aided you in managing your anxiety and sleep. Perhaps you were unable to experience any joy but felt adrift, purposeless. A prescription medication may have enabled you to get through that depressing time. If you feel your medication isn't working and you aren't getting the result you anticipated or have side effects, it's important to contact your provider right away. You may need a reduction or increase in the prescribed dosage, or you may need a completely different medication.

Before you discontinue any medication, consult with your doctor. Just because the pandemic has eased does not mean that its impact on your brain has simply gone away, far from it. You may find that the fears and concerns that circulated in your mind still bleed through. Continuing your medication for a time may require a step-down approach as you realign your body and brain to your new/old regime to provide you with a safe readjustment.

Perhaps you were already taking prescription medications

before the pandemic. You may have had to make some adjustments, perhaps increase dosages, to contend with your reactions. Now that COVID has eased, your medication needs may have changed. Again, chart your emotions. Examine your daily ups and downs, your responses to personal and social events. Do you feel that you no longer need medication? Do you now feel stable, more content with the return to "normal"? Again, consult with your provider to determine the appropriate dosages.

While it is vital to care for your mental health after the pandemic, don't forget your body. Many of you may have avoided medical check-ups beyond emergency or crises contacts. Hopefully, you continued your prescription medications during this time. Now is the time to continue with those routine doses, but it is especially important to get your annual well-person check-up. This should include bloodwork, cancer screens, and a review of any physical changes, including weight. Don't forget the dentist and the eye doctor.

Visits to providers were down during COVID, according to the Centers for Disease Control. People had postponed and, in some cases, ignored routine medical appointments. Some of this was due to limited hours and procedures offered by providers. Some of the hesitations were simply out of fear. Now we have moved away from the pandemic restrictions and, once again, can engage in medical treatment. Now is the time to revisit your personal needs and update prescriptions. Maybe it is time to clean out that medicine cabinet and remove outdated prescriptions, depositing them at a safe community site.

As you move into renewing yourself, hopefully you have an established medical provider. Perhaps not. Perhaps you moved to a new community. Perhaps your provider retired. If you do not have a current physician, now is the time to find one.

Initiating Your Medical Team

Your first visit to your regular doctor or to a new provider after COVID should include a good physical exam. Before you arrive for your appointment with a new provider, you can verify the provider's credentials and the insurance accepted and check on specialties and days and hours available. Usually, this can be accomplished on the Internet.

Once you feel comfortable and make the appointment, the next important step is to make a list of your medical problems or concerns. You might even want to journal your concerns so you don't forget when you are face to face with your provider. Be sure you take any medications with you or at least a list of them. The provider will ask. If it is your first time, they will conduct a brief medical history, including hospitalizations and surgeries. Be very specific with the provider. What is going on with your body now? Are you struggling with weight? Headaches, backaches, chronic pain? How are your sleep patterns? Are you feeling anxious or depressed?

The purpose of this section is not to analyze what a physician might say to you, but to prepare you, the patient, for the visit. I am guilty of going to the doctor with a headache lasting a week and neglecting to tell him that my knee was aching. Somehow, people have started thinking the care provider only wanted one problem a visit, which is not true, at least not for most doctors. Typically, they plan at least one annual well-person review. While billing and other factors may play a role in what occurs in a session, a caring medical provider does not want to ignore any symptoms that might create further problems for you, their patient, as you journey back to your usual life routine.

One other point about care providers, whether medical or mental, is the importance of feeling comfortable and open with them. Conscientious providers will respect your decision to change providers when you do not feel that the current one is a "good fit." Some providers have a calm bedside manner. Others may seem more distant in their approach. I like to remind patients of this because they should not feel guilty if they change providers and seek someone who has a different personality, style or use of language, or if they feel the current provider is not credible. The main concern for you, the patient, is comfort as well as quality care.

Another factor to consider when selecting a general provider is how well they integrate with the rest of your medical team. For example, you may have specialists, cardiologists, neurologists, oncologists, gynecologists, and so forth. That they can work together for the benefit of the patient is the most important factor. Other integrated providers should include dentists. Your medical provider needs to be made aware of any extensive dental procedures so that together they and your dentist can treat any symptoms or order medication as needed. Your dental provider may also need to have specific information, just as the medical provider did, which may include your dental history, what medications you are on, and, of course, any physical diagnoses or conditions that might affect your dental treatment.

Whenever you have several different providers, you may need to complete a release of information or coordination form if you want them to communicate with each other. This is required under the Health Insurance Portability and Accountability Act (HIPAA). Under this federal law, your medical information is protected from public disclosure unless you give permission.

Releases are also required for other individuals, such as family members or close friends or partners. Releases also are needed when the patient is referred by a probation or parole officer or by the department of social services. These patients are usually involved with legal problems or child or adult custody. These releases are usually completed by both the requester and the agency or individual providing the medical, dental, or mental health information. Keep in mind that releases can also be revoked. This information is valuable to you as you are assured of the privacy of your appointments and any diagnoses, medications, or care.

Medical providers often refer patients to mental health because physical and mental health problems are closely associated. If you have pains and aches, they may be strictly physical in origin. However, they may significantly contribute to your stress and anxiety, perhaps even resulting in depression. Likewise, your mental health symptoms can accentuate medical problems, resulting in the feeling of more intense pain.

Finally, the mental health (also known as behavioral health) professional needs to be part of an integrated team approach. Gone are the days, I hope, when a person was considered *crazy* if they attended therapy with a *shrink*. Today, we recognize more fully that a medical provider will be the first to note that the patient is feeling depressed or anxious. The provider may then refer the patient to a behavioral health therapist who can then follow up with an assessment and provide appropriate treatment for the patient or make other referrals, if necessary.

COVID-19 brought an outburst of varying emotions within the population, anxiety and depression being the most prevalent. For people who have experienced past trauma, those effects may have worsened due to the pandemic. These various emotions, coupled with fears and ongoing personal problems, can sometimes lead people to have thoughts of self-harm. There is no documentation that COVID itself has led to an increase in suicide among the population. Regardless, all providers, medical, dental, and mental, should be consistently aware of signs of self-harm or suicide attempts among their patients.

When providers meet with their patients, they need to be aware of the subtle ways in which these emotions are expressed. Usually, people do not come out and say, "I'm thinking about killing myself." Instead, they phrase their thoughts in different ways that their providers can sometimes ignore or bypass. In the case of COVID, they might even say, "We're all going to die from this anyway. What's the point?" I had a patient say that.

More often, the language may be in the form of a statement. For example:

"I'm so tired of living like this."
"Sometimes it just isn't worth it."
"No one would miss me if I was gone."
"I just want to go to sleep and forget it all."

Such remarks, even if they seem off-handed, should set off an alarm. Further direct questions are essential. A myth says that directly asking about suicide or suicide intent is dangerous, that it might give the patient the idea. Nothing is further from the truth. Asking direct questions can lead to saving a life. "Do you wish to be dead?"; "Are you having thoughts of killing yourself?"; "How would you do it if you killed yourself?"; "Have you worked out a plan?"; and "Have you ever tried to kill yourself before?" Continue with your questions. "How? When?" The information will be referred to a mental health provider or a psychiatrist.

If the patient answers "yes" or there is a suspicion that self-harm might happen or be happening, the provider should immediately respond with the referral to a mental health agency or an emergency room where a qualified professional will be available to assess the patient. The individuals struggling with their thoughts may then be placed on a hold or a suicide watch. The length will depend on how the person responds to key self-harm questions. If the qualified provider determines the person is not likely to self-harm, a safety plan is constructed. The person is then released to an appropriate family member or another supportive person.

If there is any doubt about the safety of the person, the professional may order a suicide watch for several days or until the patient is referred to a specialized inpatient program, where the specific level of treatment needed will be determined.

It's important to know that medical and mental health providers are not the only people responsible for spotting suicidal or homicidal thoughts in others. Sometimes it is easy to overlook those signs in the people closest to us, our family or friends. We can listen to them, let them vent, cry, and express their emotions. We can then suggest that they talk with their doctor and obtain appropriate physical and mental health assessments. We can't force people to action or into treatment, but we can reach out and make recommendations.

The bottom line is that *you* might save a life.

Your medical, dental, and behavioral health providers can act as a supportive team as you journey further from the impact of COVID toward stability. Having this integrated team behind you is invaluable, as they are also part of the valuable social network described in the next chapter.

6

Support Systems

Who would you call if your father died? Who could you depend on to help you move across town? Who do you connect with when life gets tough? Because it does. Life is often messy. These are the times when we need a friend or a support person. Perhaps nothing could demonstrate this more effectively than COVID-19 and its variants.

Psychologist Albert Ellis has written that people rarely react passively to their environments. We actively seek to interact and construct and reconstruct behavior to achieve our innate and learning goals. We need others to meet our physical and emotional needs. Even those people who shy away from others find they must reach out simply to retrieve groceries. They also require other services, such as car repairs, medical treatment, or computer repairs.

As noted earlier, some people exhibit introverted characteristics. They do not seem to require frequent social interaction. Yet, we are all social animals. We are dependent on others for many things. However, the primary way people provide strength and act as a resource is by emotional support. We need hugs and eye contact. We need people just to listen at times. Being able to pick up the phone and contact someone when your lover leaves you or the washing machine breaks down is valuable and irreplaceable.

If you are not particularly comfortable with establishing a host of friends, don't. However, I strongly recommend that you find a friend, one person you can count on when the world goes crazy. In other words, give your brain a new message that you can search for and find someone who shares some of the same interests, but mostly someone who will be with you during tough times. Yes, they may enjoy similar films and music, but they don't mind when you are quiet for a time, and they just listen. Am I suggesting that this is an easy task? Far from it. If you have been a loner most of your life, you might be fearful of rejection or that you might make a critical mistake. But finding a faithful friend is so rewarding. And I urge you to take the risk.

Other people, those extroverts, are ready for the party, the reunion, the reveal at any moment. They appear to thrive when with others. Perhaps they have 300 friends on Facebook. Even so, caution is in order. All who are classified as friends aren't always friends. Someone once told me that if we have one to two true friends in our life, that's about right. Others are acquaintances. I often think of drawing a circle, putting yourself in the middle, then close friends (maybe family members) in another circle, then others in another circle, and so on. Out there on the fringes are the least important contacts and the lower levels of acquaintances.

The reason I urge caution with selecting your friends goes back to the weeds in your garden. We need to pull them out sometimes. Who are the real friends, the ones we can count on? Who are the ones who are loyal and don't gossip about us to others? Who are those who lead us to drugs, crime, or disruptions in our relationships? I am reminded of an old saying I have often used with young people who rely too much on their peers. To paraphrase, it goes, "Show me three people you hang out with, and I will tell you where you will be in five years." Of course, that's not definitive. People sometimes change and make healthier choices as they garner life experiences. Still, it is worth examining in your life and determining if you need to weed your garden.

As you make your list of goals and changes that will improve your life after COVID, remember that making positive choices in friends and supportive people is critical for success. Am I telling you to toss out people who have problematic lives? Of course not. It is important, however, to review your association with these people and determine if they truly support you and your needs.

I am often reminded of clean and sober people who have a significant other who abuses drugs or alcohol. Sometimes they envision themselves as a role model for the other person, believing that they can demonstrate the path to success or that they can save the other person. Typically, this is not what happens. Instead, the sober person is frequently brought down by the abuser. Picking our support people takes time and an honest selection.

We all know people, possibly ourselves, who have made mistakes in their lives and ended up in jail or prison. When examining the importance of support for yourself and others, don't forget the many individuals who are still locked up. They may be family, friends, or acquaintances, but they also need encouragement during their incarceration and after their release.

Perhaps you have been a support person for a son or daughter incarcerated during COVID. Maybe a family friend was locked up, and you've been writing support letters for the past year. Knowing that people you care about may have a higher rate of exposure to COVID, you may feel more stressed and depressed. You do not want your concerns to affect your health negatively.

You also do not want to remove your support from your loved ones. They need support now and as the pandemic changes its direction, moving through variant stages and the possible need for booster shots. Research from the Equal Justice Initiative indicates that incarcerated people are at great risk of sickness and death due to COVID-19.[1]

The inability to quarantine or practice social distancing imperils the lives of many incarcerated people, who are already living in overcrowded conditions. According to the *New York Times*, as of April 16, 2021, more than 661,000 incarcerated people had been infected with coronavirus, and at least 2,990 inmates and officers had died.[2] They also reported that prisons, jails, and detention centers are "among the nation's most dangerous places when it comes to infections from the coronavirus." Inmates can only manage their reactions to the events surrounding them. They must endure the illness surrounding them, even cellmates dying.

Another concern you and your incarcerated friend may have is that vaccinations have been slower coming to prisons, and then the focus was primarily on staff. Many inmates also do not trust the justice system or have had negative experiences in medical care.

---

1. Equal Justice Initiative. 2021. "Impact on People in Prison." 16 April. https://eji.org/news/covid-19s-impact-on-peope-in-prison. Accessed 24 September 2021.

2. "Coronavirus in the U.S.: Latest Map and Case Count." 2021. *New York Times*, 16 April. https://nyti.ms/39jvJEY. Accessed 24 September 2021.

Therefore, they are very hesitant to take the vaccine. A combination of the inability to socially distance and higher rates of chronic health issues has led to prison mortality rates two to three times higher than that of the general population.[3]

One inmate shared his personal experience with COVID, noting that the virus was initially brought into his facility by employees and then "spread like wildfire." He pointed out that offenders were segregated into their housing units to stop the spread, but illness was impossible to avoid in such confined spaces. Proper personal protective equipment for staff was limited. A major concern was with some inmates who had serious medical problems and already compromised immunity. At the time of this writing, his facility is still on an "advanced level of COVID restriction." However, it is short-staffed due to some employees being ill and some refusing to be vaccinated.

As strong support for your incarcerated family and friends, you can ensure that they receive accurate information about the pandemic, including vaccinations. They may not have attended their GED classes, mental health therapy sessions, or substance abuse treatment during this time. With encouragement, they can continue to manage during their stay and move forward to a productive future.

Many of you may have family or friends who work in the correctional system.[4] Your concerns for those people, who can benefit from your ongoing support and love, are equally valuable. Making certain that they get time to relax and have work-home boundaries is essential. Spending time watching comedy programs, playing games, or simply walking with the family is vital to managing the stressors associated with their work.

If you are one of those essential workers, you need to protect yourself by separating yourself from your work or establishing boundaries. During your shifts, you may have experienced stress from loss of staff, resulting in more overtime and more security challenges. This lack of staff can result in more violence and abuse within your facility. You may have witnessed and possibly been a part of

3. Herring, Tiana, and Emily Widra. 2021. "Just Over Half of Incarcerated People Are Vaccinated, Despite Being Locked in COVID-19 Epicenters." Prison Policy Initiative, 18 May. https://www.prisonpolicy.org/blog/2021/05/18/vaccinationrates/. Accessed 24 September 2021.

4. See Gary Cornelius. 2005. *Stressed Out: Strategies for Living and Working with Stress in Corrections.* Durham: Carolina Academic Press.

violence and abuse. Because you are a compassionate person, you also may feel concern and fear for those older inmates, many with medical and mental health problems.

If you were to check data, you would find that the percentage of people in state prisons who are fifty-five and older more than tripled between 2000 and 2016, mainly due to the "tough on crime" policies for convicted felons.[5] Coupled with the increased medical problems of the older population, this creates further concern for family and friends who have been incarcerated throughout the pandemic.

If you are a correctional worker, your anxiety and fear may be further driven by your knowledge of the seriousness of the virus and your constant interaction with inmates and staff along with the lack of distancing. However, you are also in a position to provide some emotional support for your coworkers and the incarcerated population.

Remember that the majority of those locked up will be released back to their families and community. They will need more support and encouragement as they adjust to life without walls and seek to re-establish themselves within their communities.

Support systems are not just about people in our lives. Animals play a tremendous role in providing love and comfort to us humans. We often think of pets such as dogs and cats as the primary household companions. They exhibit affection by displaying happiness upon our arrival home, wagging their tail or purring, barking affectionately, cuddling and responding with enthusiasm to their meals, and let's not forget treats.

While dogs and cats are welcomed as playmates, they also serve as valuable therapeutic friends. These animals listen without judgment while we rant about the hazards of our workday. They sit on our laps, we stroke them with genuine love, and they respond with unlimited devotion. For those with mental health problems, animals can often supply comfort and aid in refocusing thoughts and recognizing gratitude in our lives. Some people obtain a certificate designating their animal, usually a dog, as a support or therapeutic animal. These animals are to be distinguished from the support

---

5. Equal Justice Initiative. 2021. "Covid-19's Impact on People in Prison." 16 April. https//eji.org/news/covid-19s-impact-on-people-in-prison. Accessed 24 September 2021.

animals used by people with medical disabilities, such as those who aid the blind and other people who are handicapped or have certain medical conditions.

In mentioning pets, I do not want to ignore other animals, such as horses, donkeys, sheep, birds, lizards, fish, gerbils, or any other animals which can provide comfort and meaning to us humans. Recently I learned that many people adopt pigs, usually smaller ones who have been neutered to keep them calmer. I know of some people who swear by their pet snakes. Not a snake lover myself. Nevertheless, I recognize the value of supportive animal relationships regardless of the species.

Animals also provide another valuable asset to people. They require that we serve them. We must fill their water bowls, open the dog or cat food and distribute it. We must provide the birdseed or the bale of hay. Let us not forget the cost of the veterinarian and yearly vaccinations. Typically, we purchase a variety of treats, including clothing and toys. All of this activity and all of these expenses keep us busy being responsible pet parents. We have a reason to get up in the morning and open the dog food. We all need a purpose.

Animals are a crucial part of the world we live in, whether they are pets or live in the wild. Just to view them in their environment, either in person or on television, opens the wonders of nature to us, a spiritual bond that provides healing insight into self.

As humans, we can reach out for support in other ways, such as aligning ourselves with a group. Locating a group that shares similar problems, medical conditions, or interests can provide an acknowledgment that "you are not alone." Meeting with them and sharing positive interactions can often open doors, not only for new rewarding associations but for self-improvement and growth. Groups such as Alcoholics Anonymous and Narcotics Anonymous, Mothers Against Drunk Driving, domestic violence support groups, Alzheimer's support groups, and numerous other groups offer education and opportunities for sharing experiences. Your local houses of worship and religious organizations and their leaders are strong support, which will be discussed further in the next chapter.

Other groups can provide us with a sense of sharing, such as charities like the Shriners, hospitals like St. Jude's, and groups focused on animal rights, medical conditions, the environment, or social issues projects. You can align yourself with and make donations to groups of your own choice. By connecting with charities, you can improve your sense of self-worth. You do not always have to donate but giving your time or wearing an arm band lets others know of the organization and your involvement with it.

Still other groups and their members often provide emotional and therapeutic support. For example, AARP, which focuses on providing benefits and support for retired people, offers lists of free support groups and programs offering tech, fitness and mindfulness tools, among other things. In addition, you might consider groups related to your hobbies, such as crocheting and quilting organizations, art groups, book clubs and gaming groups. The list is endless. The important thing is to pick an organization that fits your interests and can be helpful to you as you progress in breaking old habits and changing your mindset, especially if you are supportive of their interests and needs.

Trust

A key to developing your support team with individuals, groups, and teams relies on one factor: trust. But just what is trust? The word *trust* may be interpreted differently by different people. It includes many concepts necessary to engage with others effectively. First of all, you must feel safe interacting with others. The pandemic has significantly impacted that safety factor. Wearing a mask and keeping your distance from loved ones sliced through that trust. Could you believe all the information conveyed as facts about COVID? And later, when the vaccines arrived, did you trust that they worked and worry about how effective they were?

The pandemic has brought with it a form of paranoia. Someone looks at you a certain way and you feel attacked, not physically, but judged and found wanting. You may also feel that you can't trust others. The news programs lie to you, the medical experts contend with each other. Confusion reigns. Who can you believe? You can't help but wonder when you wipe every doorknob and counter in your home and are still unsure if you are safe. What about the food you brought from the store?

We extend trust to others by our body language and by our voice and how we hold ourselves when interacting. Yet, with the critical importance of wearing masks, we no longer could see a smile, except in the eyes. We no longer shook hands and embraced. Just how were we to demonstrate and reciprocate trust under these circumstances?

When COVID began to feel less threatening, you may have managed to subdue those initial fears. But how do you rebuild trust, especially with family, friends, and neighbors? I suggest you begin with baby steps. Think of trust as a bank account. Before the pandemic, most of us had a certain amount of trust toward others, our medical providers, the grocery store, the auto mechanic, and, of course, friends and family. The account was bursting. Then along came the pandemic, and suddenly all the funds in your account were drained.

To build that account back up requires time, patience, and work. You must develop those baby steps that will work for you, often one step at a time. What was the last joke you told? Perhaps it is time to tell one to a friend and to roar with laughter. You need to participate in an activity that will open those doors to trust once more. Trust includes feeling like you are being heard and that others are exhibiting integrity toward you, that they are dependable, and that you are not being judged, confronted, or attacked by others. You must exhibit those same qualities to others. Again, this may take time and effort.

Rebuilding your trust account is critical if you truly want to use your support systems and support others in your life. Re-establishing trust is critical if you are to bounce back from the pandemic in a healthy manner. However, a major barrier to success is often failed communication. By examining communication factors in the next chapter, you may be able to sustain relationships positively.

7

Communication

What is communication anyway? It is a way of giving or exchanging information through ideas, thoughts, feelings, and attitudes—verbally or nonverbally. Verbal, of course, refers to the use of words. Nonverbal focuses on body movement and includes eye contact, gestures, posture, head motion, touch, facial expressions, overall appearance, and how near to or far away we are from the other person. Some experts say that body language comprises the majority of our communication. For example, using body language during a job interview can instantly provide a favorable impression. Conversely, it might cost you a desired promotion.

With the social changes resulting from COVID-19, communication was profoundly affected. Many people began working from home, providing services through video or telephone. In some cases, this may have interfered with body language or distorted our words. Other people may have lost jobs, needing to polish their communication skills to locate other ways of earning income. Communication may have been silenced at times because people were forced to use masks in public that restricted their eye, head, and facial movements. The importance of exchanging information accurately was never more evident than in the pandemic.

Whether you are using verbal or nonverbal communication, understanding others and conveying good information depends largely on your communication style. Knowing your style and that of others can aid in building stronger relationships.

There are four different basic communication styles: passive, aggressive, passive-aggressive, and assertive. Take a look at the following brief descriptions of these styles and zero in on which style you believe fits you.

Passive individuals often fail to express their feelings, opinions, wants or needs. Typically, they avoid confrontations and display poor eye contact and a slumped body posture. They tend to speak softly or apologetically and often allow others to deliberately or inadvertently infringe on their rights. The impact of this style is that they may feel anxiety; their life may seem out of control. They may experience depression because they feel stuck. They often ignore their feelings, which can lead them to feel resentful and confused at times. A passive person may say or believe they have no power and are continually being stepped on by others.

If you are a passive person, how will you act or behave if the boss asks you to work overtime? Most probably, you will lower your eyes and shift your shoulders. Then, you would meekly respond with something like, "Sure, no problem." Inside, you are churning. You wanted to watch the Monday night playoff game. Still, there's nothing you can do about it. Or is there?

If you are a passive person, you are likely also an introvert. When the pandemic struck, you most likely accepted closing your office and going home. With the passage of months and the introduction of vaccines, you responded to the information with little fuss. As the Delta and Omicron variants arose, you accepted the company, state, or federal mandates once more.

Passive people can be easy to get along with. They desire to be liked and recognized for their positive qualities, leading them to keep the peace at their own expense. True, they are often well organized and steady workers, and they focus well to achieve their goals. However, the downside is that their frustrations tend to build up like a pressure cooker. Because they do not let off steam, at some point, often a minor trigger, they are likely to explode. Of course, they feel guilty and ashamed and will probably apologize, and the cycle begins anew.

Aggressive individuals are typically extroverts. They usually act in a dominating manner, using a loud voice, demanding, blaming, and threatening others while displaying intense eye contact. They often criticize or attack others verbally and sometimes physically and are rude and impulsive with a low frustration level. They may be violating the rights of others while advocating for themselves. They may speak loudly and in a demanding manner, even displaying threatening motions with their body language. They may point their fingers at other people when in disagreement, using "you" statements. In addition, they interrupt often and are not patient listeners. Aggressive people typically believe that they are superior and entitled, and others who challenge them are wrong. They think they have a right to intimidate and dominate others.

As a result of these behaviors, they may become alienated from other people. By generating fear and hatred in others, they probably have fewer friends or support people in their life. They typically blame others instead of owning their issues and appear unable to mature and take responsibility for their behaviors.

If you were an aggressive person, how would you react when the boss asked you to work overtime? Most probably, you would say, as you shifted your weight around, lifting your shoulders in a threatening manner, "Nope. Can't do it. I got plans. Make Mike do it." If pushed, you might say, "How much you gonna pay me?"

When the pandemic struck, aggressive people were most likely to become angry and hostile when told to go home and shelter in place. These personalities did not take kindly to a mask, outright refusing at times to wear one. They may have insisted that it was all a hoax or blamed China or the government or believed in conspiracy theories. Even as COVID appeared to wane, they continued to post negative messages and refused the vaccine. As the Delta variant took hold, further protests and curses probably exploded from their lips.

Aggressive personalities can be strong leaders because of their powerful nature. They appear confident and outgoing. In the workplace, they may champion ideas, especially if they are passionate about a cause. They also have few problems approaching their leaders.

Passive-aggressive individuals usually appear calm and cooperative on the outside, but they are often angry and seething inside. They may complete a task cooperatively but then spread rumors and sabotage the efforts of others. This subtle and indirect manner makes them outwardly appear easy-going and pleasant to others, while they are incapable of dealing with their objections and feelings openly. As a result, they often procrastinate.

Typically, they have difficulty acknowledging their anger and may use facial expressions that don't match their real feelings. They may mutter to themselves rather than confront the issue or person. As a result of their behaviors, they may become alienated from others and remain stuck in a feeling of powerlessness. Because they don't address the issues or feelings, they display resentment and try to "get even" with others.

The passive-aggressive person may believe he is powerless and feel uncertain about how to handle this feeling. Yet inside he wants to react. They often are like snipers, who stand behind a barrier and take potshots at the enemy.

If you are a passive-aggressive person, how would you respond when the boss asked you to work late? Most probably, you would comply. You might say, "Sure, no problem." That's your passive mode. But inside, you are seething. You also wanted to watch Monday night football. As a result, you decide you'll get even. As you render your saw, you cut each board two inches short. They won't discover it until tomorrow.

This getting even and sabotaging your company can also result in dire consequences for yourself. In the meantime, you text your friends and explain to them how demanding and inconsiderate your boss is.

When the pandemic struck, just like a passive person, most probably you accepted it, shrugged your shoulders and went home. But when you got home, you began ranting at the boss, your company, the stupid government. You may have thrown a dish or two in frustration. Then as COVID progressed through vaccination and even to this date, you may have taken the events in stride but then reacted in angry outbursts.

We might all demonstrate passive-aggressive traits at times. If the behavior is interfering with relationships, family, work or social events, a trained professional can administer tests and provide therapy to aid the persons in modifying their behaviors.

Assertive individuals reflect the most effective type of communication. These individuals can openly express their needs and wants while validating the feelings of others. They communicate openly and respectfully and take ownership of their feelings and behaviors without blaming others. They demonstrate a relaxed body posture and speak calmly and clearly while feeling competent and in control.

They communicate respect for others and use "I" statements instead of pointing the finger making "you" accusations.

They create a respectful environment for others around them; they feel more connected to others and more in control. Because they address issues and problems as they arise, they are less anxious or stressed and can convey those pleasant feelings to other associates.

Assertive people behave in a manner that suggests confidence. They have an understanding that they can't control others but can control themselves. They can get their needs met productively and respectfully and know that they are completely responsible for their happiness.

Imagine yourself as an assertive individual. How are you going to respond when the boss asks you to work late? You might state, "I would love to help you out, but I have a family night planned. Is it possible that I could come in early in the morning and finish that project?" By doing this, you are demonstrating respect for yourself and the company. You are offering an alternative so that the job gets completed. The boss may or may not use this option, but he is more likely to listen.

Under which communication style are you more likely to get your needs and wants met? If you have identified your style, journal your responses and list how you might be able to modify and improve yourself. A positive goal would be to move closer to the assertive style to enjoy more effective communication with family, friends, and co-workers.

Remember that communication can be accomplished in various ways—by speaking, writing, creating art, making music, dancing, or using technology. A key factor is language. Therefore, your first consideration should be actual language. For example, if a person doesn't speak English, is an interpreter needed to convey the exact meaning? Remember that words do not always translate exactly from one language to another. If you reside in an area with a large percentage of Spanish-speaking residents, you may need someone to translate. I have known children to translate for their parents, a wonderful experience for all concerned.

Also important is to consider regional accents. My family came from the Deep South. When my ear hears the warm rhythms, I sometimes have to pause to garner the full meaning. Words like "You all" become “Y’all,” a very poetic pull-together, which is an illustration of how, in our own country, from east to west, north to south, dialects may differ. Sometimes, even when watching a movie, we may not always understand if the characters speak with a British or Italian accent. Those beautiful, musical Irish brogues often lend themselves to misunderstandings.

And what about slang? Slang is defined as informal and unofficial language. Often slang originates with cultural groups and becomes part of the common language through assimilation and appropriation. However, some slang derives from historic events, like “going nuclear,” or entertainment, such as “warp drive.” Slang can vary greatly from generation to generation. Older people often have a more traditional use of the language, perhaps more proper English. Yet, they, too, may have their own slang. In the ’50s, people used words like “cooler” and “boo-boo.” The ’70s brought “no brainer” and “threads,” while in the ’90s we heard words like “bling” and “dead presidents,” a reference to paper money. And how many times have we heard “good” turned into “bad”? Remember that the first English-speaking settlers in America probably thought any word not used in Britain was slang!

Of course, people sometimes develop their secret languages or codes, which are generally confined to select groups. We often associate codes with war as governments attempt to tap into relevant military plans or the development of emerging technology. During the formation of the United States, code breakers were used to determine battle plans of the enemy.

Communication has taken many forms over the centuries, affording greater accessibility to those individuals with special needs. From the first recorded use of sign language in the 5th century to today’s American Sign Language (ASL), this tool has opened valuable interaction among many people. We can also thank Louis Braille for his invention, a means of reading and writing for the blind. With the invention in 1964 of the TTY machine, also known as TDD, people with other disabilities were able to be included in the communication. Today with the further improvement of electronic devices, such as special computers, printers, and phones, services for all folks regardless of disability have improved.

The use of e-mail and texting has added entirely new definitions to words, creating new words, abbreviations and images to express emotions and ideas. For example, the simple "CU" means "see you" and "LOL" means "laughing out loud." These are but a couple of examples of SMS language (text language). These shortcuts were devised to aid users of early phones, where typing a message was difficult. Today's smartphones are much easier, but the SMS language still cuts typing time.

People can now insert emojis or small digital images or icons in their communication to express ideas. An example is a sad face, which depicts sadness, anger, worry, and numerous other emotions. In addition, people are adding personal avatars to their Facebook and Messenger applications. An avatar is an individual's virtual lookalike with expressions, along with a variety of clothing, equipment, and seasonal and special sayings.

In our own lives, if uncertain, we really should not repeat what we thought we heard or read, whether it is spoken or written. If we do not understand, are confused or misled, passing along messages can lead to disagreements, conflicts, and disruptions in our relationships. During the COVID pandemic, such misunderstandings surfaced in social media and were evident in family disruptions. The inability to manage conflict is a major factor in the severance of relationships.

Conflict Management

When we think of communication, we often refer to *talking* and how meaning is conveyed in that manner. Speaking face to face shows our expressions, body language, and others can hear our tone and emphasis on words. It can demonstrate affection or hatred. It can be a tool for embracing or for distancing. Words are powerful. How we use or not use them can be the difference between understanding and cementing relationships or destroying them.

Meaningful communication is critical in relationships and conflict resolution. The ability to manage conflict is probably one of the biggest hurdles in relationships. People who cannot manage conflict argue often and fight much of the time, leading to domestic violence situations and even police and court intervention.

During the pandemic, you may have been sharing your residence with a spouse, loved one, or another member of your family. Close quarters, differences in viewpoints, loss of work, and realigning household duties can all stretch tension. Some conflict is natural when we interact with people, especially those we love. The outcome of that conflict depends on how we handle our responses.

Personality styles play a huge role in how people manage their emotions with their spouses, partners, and children. When you initially sheltered in place with your family, you may have discovered that even "small things" could begin to irritate you. You rubbed against each other frequently. Something as simple as an undercooked hamburger could send you into a rage. Recall the first chapter when an examination of styles revealed the importance of responding or reacting. These styles are very important when we review the role of domestic violence during COVID.

If you are a passive person, chances are you allowed others to "walk all over you." You withdrew and quietly "obeyed" the instructions or demands of the other person. However, if you are more aggressive, most probably you gave the orders and, when your mate didn't follow through quickly, you raised your voice, making demands. As an assertive person, you tried to use calm language and a caring demeanor with yourself and your family through the pandemic as you eased into the variant stage.

As requirements around COVID continue to alter and the pandemic takes on different phases, it is extremely important to recognize what comprises domestic violence. Some people think that if they haven't struck their partner or children, they aren't committing a crime. However, the law says differently. While some states may have varying definitions and standards around domestic violence, the categories remain consistent.

Physical violence: This includes striking, slapping, burning, twisting an arm, pulling hair, choking, kicking, and shoving. Physical violence usually begins with angry words and then rapidly escalates unless the victims give in to the abusers or escape or unless the perpetrators gain control of their emotions and remove themselves from the scene. A simple argument can rapidly turn violent. A tragedy occurred when a woman held her newborn child and her husband struck her in the face. The child flew out of her arms, landed violently against a cabinet, and was killed.

Sexual violence: Sexual violence includes rape. Many men do not realize that marital rape is a form of domestic violence. I once met a man in prison who was serving five years as a result of this crime. He learned his wife had had sex with another man, and, in his rage, he attacked her. Date rape is another form of sexual violence. An attacker, typically male of greater size and strength, finalizes a pleasant evening with expectations of sex. When his date refuses, his anger turns violent.

Sexual violence also includes sexual harassment or offending a person sexually or using sex as a punishment. The boss who continually demands sex from his assistant under threat of job loss is guilty of this behavior. Another example is the man who refers to his partner as a "whore" or a "slut" as a controlling mechanism.

Verbal abuse: Verbal abuse includes words that are used to control or hurt another person. Almost all family violence begins verbally and then escalates to physical violence. With couples and families spending so much time together during the pandemic, words could easily and thoughtlessly get hurled at each other. An example is the wife who berates her husband with condemning words such as "You're such a bastard! You just want to blame COVID. You could find a job. You're just a lazy SLOB!" Or the man who yells at his wife, "Get off that damned Internet! You don't need that class. It just costs us money. Shut down now!"

Emotional or psychological abuse: This category includes physical and verbal abuse. Typically, one person attempts to exercise power and control over another person. They deny the other person the opportunity to make their own choices and often dictate who they see and where they go. They withhold love and finances to get their demands met.

The fear that someone will physically harm or leave us keeps many people in dangerous and abusive relationships and situations. An example is a man who constantly checks the messages on his wife's phone because he believes she is cheating. In his jealous rage, he may call her names and say, "I know you're sleeping with him!" He may move from emotional abuse to violence. His constant haranguing can result in her experiencing elevated anxiety, depression, or suicidal ideations.

As the pandemic emerged and families were thrust together

with few opportunities for separate activities, emotions were often pushed to the limit. Many people lost their jobs and were impacted severely, unable to pay for their housing and groceries. Family stress, anxiety, and even depression increased. Used to supporting their family and feeling useful, parents experience boredom and a loss of purpose and identity. Sheltering in place often contributed to partners blaming each other for their problems.

Compounding the issues, they were now required to homeschool their children. The children were continually underfoot, bringing their anger and squabbles into the open. In addition, in many cases, the parents now had to familiarize themselves with more difficult technology. Some people realized that their children's homework had advanced beyond their capability. The tools, techniques, and curriculum were vastly different.

With partners consistently linked together, they had few breaks in the initial stages of COVID, which meant that all those "little things" that previously may have irritated each other now came to the front. Simple chores, like sorting the laundry or doing the dishes, became open to inspection and micromanaging by their partner.

During times of disaster, domestic violence rates have tended to increase. Because of the extended period of this pandemic, many experts believe the rates may be even greater than in past crises. As COVID appeared to level out and the Delta variant arose, further stress and animosity arose, contributing to more arguments and abuse in family systems.

A major concern of many domestic violence treatment centers has been the "stay at home" mandate, which protects the public and can contribute to the increase in violence. For example, victims may be forced to spend more time with their abusers, who have greater opportunities to engage in power and control behaviors.

Social distancing measures can prevent victims from seeking help and stifle their ability to leave. Some reports indicate that perpetrators have provided misinformation to their partners to keep them from medical care, withholding items like hand sanitizer or telling their partners they have COVID to ensure the partner remains with them.

Attempting to provide counseling or therapy to the victim became more difficult. With the use of telehealth, problems with confidentiality arose. Is the perpetrator listening? Will he retaliate against the victim after the call? The use of safety plans created another issue, with the victim's options of leaving home and putting the changes in social supports at risk.[1]

Nevertheless, many counselors developed processes to aid victims in their homes. Some asked questions with "yes" or "no" answers to determine if the person was alone before continuing, then inquired about needs but proceeding with care, listening, inquiring, enhancing safety, referring to appropriate services, and establishing a safe follow-up.

As the pandemic has eased, concerns still exist about the variants, vaccines, and future requirements. Learning new communication skills, regardless of outside events or personal frustrations, is critical to maintaining stability and contentment in your life.

The importance of managing conflict applies to all members of a household. If you believe you are or have been a victim of domestic violence at any time, not just during the pandemic, it's important to reach out to a counselor, therapist, support group, or medical provider. If you are fearful that you might abuse a partner, child, or anyone else, or if you have done so, it is not too late to learn coping and communication skills. You, too, should reach out to protect your loved ones and yourself from any potential danger.

As you review your stressors in this constricted environment during COVID, it is an excellent time to revert to your journal and document some of the conflicts you experienced. You may have bottled up those feelings to the point that they resulted in losing your temper and taking your frustrations out on others.

Unrealistic Expectations

One of the greatest contributors to conflict is unrealistic expectations. This refers to the idea that the world, events, and people around us should appear and act in a specific manner. For example, a man perceives that the household duties should all fall on his wife. He becomes very angry when she does not conform to these expectations.

---

1. Neil, Jennifer. 2020. "Domestic Violence and Covid-19: Our Hidden Epidemic." *Australian Journal of General Practice* 49 (June 11). https://www1.racgp.org.au/ajgp/coronavirus/domestic-violence-and-covid-19.

Or perhaps, after twenty years of marriage, a woman believes that her husband should still weigh 175 pounds. When he tips the scale at 225, she becomes increasingly angry, grouchy, and argumentative. Perhaps we expect our boss to listen to and adopt all of our suggestions. When he doesn't, we bad-mouth him to other employees.

When we have unrealistic expectations, we believe that people, organizations and systems should bend to our wants and needs. When they do not live up to these expectations, we can experience frustration and anger and even react physically.

An unrealistic expectation around COVID might be that you thought it would be over in a couple of weeks. You could pack up your briefcase and head back to the office. When that didn't happen, you may have projected your anger onto the government, the Centers for Disease Control, or your company. And it was easy to vent to your spouse, to make threats, or to refuse to follow any of the recommendations for preventing contamination.

The pandemic has resulted in many other responses. You may have expected that your family and friends should all react the way you did. When they refused to wear masks or get vaccinated, you might have become angry, sullen, unwilling to communicate respectfully with them. Perhaps you slammed them on Facebook or cut off interaction. This communication breakdown did not need to occur. Adjusting our expectations and learning to manage conflict with kindness and compassion provides the key to positive relationships.

The truth is that few people have had direct training in conflict management. It is not a subject taught in grade school. Instead, most of us resort to behavior and habits learned from our families while growing up and we often resort to non-productive resolutions. These methods of communication usually fail to solve problems. They can create more arguing and greater division.

As you work on improving your communication skills, avoid using the following tactics.

Non-Productive Resolutions

Avoidance: This means just walking away from a disagreement, even over the pandemic, refusing to discuss the problem or listen to another person's viewpoint. Or it might include just hammering away and spouting your views until the other person gives up.

Force: Force can include physical and emotional force. The person who "wins" is the one who exerts the most force, calling others names or threatening them because they disagree with one's viewpoint.

Minimization: This means making light of the situation or the other person's feelings, such as insisting that COVID is just another kind of flu, even when your partner gets sick.

Blame: Blaming someone else for the conflict can temporarily relieve some guilt. You might blame the unmasked person who made you sick, China or the government for false information.

Silencing: This is stopping the other person from sharing information by crying, yelling, screaming, or pretending to get sick. Your partner tries to convey her fears about the pandemic, but you yell, pretending you are too sick to talk and lock yourself in your room.

Gunnysacking: You store up complaints, and when the next disagreement occurs, you pull them out of the bag and confront the other person with all the stored up "wrongs." When your partner disagrees about the pandemic, you remind him about talking to his ex on the phone and losing that job last year and on and on it goes.

Manipulation: This is diverting attention by acting charming or receptive so that the "stronger" person wins the disagreement. When your partner complains that you are not working now and need to help with the chores, you put your arms around her, smile, call her "sweetie," and vow to do better.

Rejection: You may withhold love and affection and, yes, sex until you get your way. You may act cold and uncaring. Your love is contingent upon you getting your way. "If you're going to believe all that leftist stuff on TV, you can sleep on the couch!"

No resolution is possible if one acts in these ways. Conflict and disruption will continue. However, positive communication can assist in resolving disagreements and arguments and in finding solutions. You can do this by employing productive conflict resolution. The following suggestions can contribute to more harmonious relationships.

Productive Conflict Resolution

Fight above the belt: Refuse to fight dirty. Avoid causing hostility and resentment. Keep your remarks gentle and respectful. Perhaps you disagree about the origin of COVID-19. You can actually "agree to disagree" and recognize the futility of wasting energy and time on petty disagreements.

Fight actively: This does not mean physically fighting, but rather remaining open-minded and participatory, with no interrupting and hearing the other person out. One suggested process is to sit down together over a cup of coffee and discuss the issue in a calm, relaxed manner.

Take responsibility for your part: Own your thoughts and feelings. Admit if you have over-reacted. Perhaps your partner has a valid point—you haven't been sharing chores since the pandemic started. Do not blame anyone else. Ask how you can remedy the situation in the future.

Be direct and specific: Focus on the here and now. Avoid situations and feelings that occurred in the past. With the advent of COVID, it is especially important to stick to the issue and focus on observable behavior. Avoid mind-reading. When we make remarks like "I know she doesn't love me anymore," we cannot see into the other person's heart. Make sure such remarks are "camera checkable." Unless she tells you that she doesn't love you, you cannot assume her emotions or thoughts.

Use humor for relief, never for ridicule: Humor can be healing. An appropriate joke or laughing at yourself or a situation can sometimes break the social ice with others. The word "appropriate" is critical. What is funny to one person may signal frustration to others. Some humor can be crude and offensive. While humor can offer a positive communication skill, it's important to know the other person's boundaries or limitations.

Laughing at yourself can provide a reality check that we all need at times. However, sometimes people sarcastically use humor to embarrass another person. That can make the conflict worse. But used in a healthy fashion, humor can provide a break in the tension. One can find jokes and humorous accounts related to the pandemic on television, the Internet, and on podcasts. Sharing these with our family and friends can help distract us. To cultivate positive social interaction, recognizing this difference in productive versus non-productive resolution is critical. The goal is to engage in meaningful communication.

Meaningful Communication

But just what comprises meaningful communication? The following is an extended list to assist you as you continue to improve your interaction with others, especially family and close friends.

Engage in good eye contact. During the pandemic, good eye contact was essential. We could not smile with our mouth, but certainly, our eyes could smile, acknowledge others, and demonstrate our moods. Continue to visually engage when it is culturally appropriate, which tells your listener that you are open to their remarks and contributions.

Openly discuss a mutual problem with ground rules. No problem can be resolved unless we open up a truthful dialogue. If you are experiencing a problem in your marriage, for example, a discussion is essential to find a solution. Ground rules include no screaming, yelling, blaming and, of course, no physical interaction. Allow no "old baggage." Decide together what is the one essential problem to discuss during this meeting.

Use gentle and reassuring language. Using soft voices goes a long way toward keeping communication pleasant, even in difficult situations. Recognizing the strengths and positive qualities of the other person paves the way to better understanding. Avoid cussing or using language that you know is offensive to the other person. Such remarks only stifle progress.

Accept the other person's point of view. No two people see the world in the same way. Our past experiences and education, our personalities and our characteristics all mold us differently. Even twins often argue over their variations in likes and dislikes, politics, religion, school, and how they view others. This divergence in viewpoints is no more evident than in the pandemic. But mature people should be able to accept another person's viewpoint, even if they heartily disagree. To do so respectfully is essential if you are engaging in a productive discussion.

Listen without interrupting. People often talk over each other. Just watch almost any film involving a conversation and you will hear the overlapping of words, sometimes to the detriment of reaching any conclusive agreement. Letting the other person finish a statement, even if they are ranting, allows you to gather your responses rationally and logically.

Clarify words and meaning if you are unsure. Words are powerful but easily misunderstood. Some words have a variety of meanings or interpretations. And what about slang words or words that are generational, as noted earlier? If your teen tosses out a favorite phrase, does it make sense to you? And if you've ever been the recipient of a garbled cell phone message, you recognize the frustration of not getting a clear message. The same is true when you are talking with someone face to face. Clarify the words and meaning if in doubt.

Repeat information. Repetition goes hand in hand with clarification. If you are unsure of your new thingamajig's price and expiration date, you better go back to the instructions. Even in our daily discussions with friends, if anyone is uncertain of what time and where we are meeting, repeat.

Plan ahead on serious discussions. Serious discussions, especially with significant others, require planning. What exactly is the point of the conversation? If there's a problem, do you have a solution or an idea for resolution? In this case, sitting down with a paper and pen and writing out what you want to say and how to say it can be beneficial. Anticipate the other person's responses and your reactions. You might want to practice the scenario ahead of time.

Use "I" language. One of the causes of anger in social interaction is "you" language, which occurs when we make accusatory remarks. For example, remarking to a friend, "If you would just quit borrowing money from me, we wouldn't fight like this" only brings defensive actions. Consider saying, "I am worried about your budget. Is there some way I can help you?" This statement might not solve the problem, but it would take the heat off the other person and perhaps open the door to a more tactful discussion.

Request, not order. Making demands on others can raise their rebellious nature, especially adolescents. Instead of ordering someone to "take the trash out right now," saying something as simple as "Hey, I'd appreciate it if you'd take the trash out before supper." Then be sure and say "Thank you" when they have completed the job.

Avoid criticism. Even when it's constructive, most of us dislike criticism. Using positive words and showing appreciation for the other person's contributions is a more productive way to begin a conversation. Communicating what adjustments might result in improvement can create more positive relationships.

Respect and compliment the other person. Along with delivering healthy criticism, complimenting the other person when appropriate aids in cementing kindness and care in any social relationship. Again, recognizing and respecting differences of opinion with others can result in a positive interaction.

Use "magic words." At times it's easy to disagree with others, especially on "hot" topics like politics and religion. Certainly, conflicts even arise on whose turn it is to do the dishes or sort the laundry. Many of us were isolated with family members during the pandemic, and it was not unusual for someone to "get on your nerves." Trying to remain cool under such circumstances might have been a challenge for you. How do we turn our feelings around so that we don't become enemies with people we love? One way is to use those magic words. Magic words consist of phrases such as "You might be right" or "I never thought of it that way." Other words could be "I'd like to think about that tonight" or "That's a good point." When uttered, these words can turn a conversation around. However, they must be said with sincerity of voice and tone and a pleasant follow-up.

Apologize when appropriate. Admitting when we are wrong or accepting that we made a mistake or misjudged someone or a situation goes a long way to healing misunderstanding. Being open and honest and selecting a positive atmosphere and mood when we apologize is essential to building stronger social skills.

Listen! Developing support systems and maintaining those systems requires healthy communication. But too often, we think of that as talking only. Yet, perhaps the most important part of communication is listening. Good quality listening is essential for quality interaction. Without listening, it is almost impossible to maintain productive communication. Just as the talking over each other interferes, so does the failure to clarify. Criticizing without hearing the other person out and allowing distractions to prevent hearing legitimate conversation all stand in the way of social interactions.

Today people are frequently distracted by their electronic devices. While scanning their e-mail and messages, they don't hear the excitement of their son's home run or the joy in their daughter's perfect grade in English. Listening is essential to positively cementing our relationships. We want to guard against such detractions.

When examining the role of support systems, I encourage you to examine your spiritual and religious convictions and values closely. Understanding the beliefs and ethics of others can provide the key to how you interact with others in your life. The next chapter will provide guidance as you look at how your convictions hold tremendous value for renewing the trust and joy in your life following the pandemic.

8

Spiritual and Religious Support

What belief system fits and is right for you? Throughout history, humans have struggled with understanding their purpose and explaining the events occurring in the world around them. Why did my child die? What caused the earthquake? Why do I long for love, and why am I sometimes disappointed? Philosophers, students, poets, and sages have pondered such questions for centuries. People have developed spiritual and religious beliefs that provide explanations and fulfill their longings.

As humans, we exist in our bodies, but we also have a mind within our bodies. We have a built-in longing for an understanding of ourselves and comprehension of the events and circumstances of our existence. These feelings persist, forming a triad of **body**, **mind**, and **spirit**.

To cast the COVID pandemic aside and truly integrate back into society, one must be attentive to all three components of our being. The importance of caring for your body has already been covered. Your body also includes your mind. Monitoring and observing your mental health is vital to functioning in a coherent and balanced manner. The third portion of the triad, the spirit, forms the crux of our values, beliefs, and potential.

For much of recorded history, the human race has attributed much of its existence to a god or gods. Those beliefs have provided sustenance during times of sorrow, disaster, and loss. These belief systems have also given birth to hope, joy, and survival. Our beliefs affect the way we ward off the fear of death. Many people have faith in an afterlife and believe that this short time on Earth is not the end of our existence or that of our loved ones.

Some people are led either by family traditions or their search toward specific beliefs, including certain religions or places of worship. These interactions provide an opportunity for bonding and meaningful social interactions with others who believe as we do. These individuals and the rituals of our faith provide support. Many people believe a higher power cares and leads people to manage difficult life circumstances.

During the pandemic, with all the craziness and seeming inconsistencies that people have been exposed to, having a shoulder to lean on, the "man upstairs," or an omniscient being or beings is a safety net. For many people, their reliance on their faith gets them through another day and provides strength and hope for the future.

Other people do not rely so much on a specific god but look to their spiritual values. They may find strength through their beliefs in nature, the stars, the magnificence of the universe, the wonders of science, or an Eastern philosophy or New Age spirituality. Whether one adheres to a specific religion or a spiritual belief, such views contain an essence of faith in something greater than oneself.

Definitions

While concepts of spirituality and religion provide meaning and purpose to one's life, there are differences between the two.

The word *spirituality* is derived from the Latin root *spiritus*, which means *breath of life*. The concept of the spirit includes ideas of wind, breath, vigor, and courage. The Summit on Spirituality and Wellness defined spirituality as an innate and unique capacity to move individuals toward knowledge, love, meaning, peace, hope, transcendence, connectedness, compassion, wellness, and wholeness.[1]

Most psychologists see spiritual development as a normal part of the human development process. Various theories exist regarding how individuals experience spiritual growth. Some models examine a stage-by-stage process, while others propose a continual process of

1. Association for Spiritual, Ethical, and Religious Values in Counseling. n.d. http://www.servic.org/spiritual-and-religious-competencies/. Accessed 22 September 2021.

growth. Regardless, the primary consideration in treatment or personal development should focus on a person's physical, emotional, and environmental dimensions.

The word religion is from the Latin word *religio,* which means a bond between humanity and greater-than-human power. The terms religion and spirituality are often used interchangeably. However, they are two separate concepts that often overlap. Some research indicates that most people (74 percent and 88 percent) do not distinguish between the two.[2]

Spirituality is a personal connection with the universe, whereas religion is an organized community of faith with a written doctrine and codes that regulate behavior.[3] People can be both religious and spiritual. To these individuals, religion and spirituality are intertwined and strengthen each other. Recognizing that our friends and neighbors hold many different views that may contrast with ours is essential to our personal development.

For example, some people may be religiously tolerant and indifferent. Others may be tolerant of others' beliefs but not committed to organized religion. Still others are religiously agnostic. They may be spiritual but have negative feelings toward organized religion. Regardless of the different perspectives toward religion or spiritual beliefs, the key to bouncing back from the pandemic in a healthy manner is examining our own beliefs and values. If you had a close family member or friend die from COVID, your religious beliefs might have been challenged, and you need to consider your approach to your religion and see if it provides meaning and comfort.

Perhaps it may be helpful for you to take a closer look at some of the positive and negative aspects of spirituality and religion as you review your own beliefs and journey toward stability and balance in your life. The Islamic 13th-century poet Rumi has a unique view on the role of religion:

> Not Christian or Jew or Muslim, not Hindu, Buddhist, Sufi, or Zen. Not any religion or cultural system. I am not from the East or the West, not out of the ocean or up from the ground, not natural or ethereal, not composed of

---

2. Cashwell, C.S., and J.S. Young. 2020. *Integrating Spirituality and Religion into Counseling; A Guide to Competent Practice, 3rd ed.* Alexandria, VA: American Counseling Association.

3. *Ibid.*

elements at all. I do not exist, am not an entity in this world or the next, did not descend from Adam or Eve or any origin story. My place is placeless, a trace of the traceless. Neither body or soul. I belong to the beloved, have seen the two worlds as one and that one call to and know, first, last, outer, inner, only that breath breathing human being.

Research indicates that one's beliefs have a significant impact on both physical and mental health outcomes. Negative spiritual beliefs align with poorer health outcomes, while positive spiritual beliefs are related to better health outcomes. A study of 200 individuals revealed that individuals with a wide range of health problems with negative spiritual beliefs had poorer physical and mental health outcomes and an increased perception of pain. Those who held positive spiritual beliefs had better outcomes and a decreased perception of pain.[4]

Examples of negative beliefs include seeing crises as punishments from God. Some people might believe this is true of COVID. This belief is similar to one held by our ancestors, who believed that God brought about natural disasters like earthquakes or volcanic eruptions. Some COVID vaccine refusers might think taking a vaccine indicates a lack of faith. They think they should rely on faith alone for protection.

Negative ideas about religious or spiritual beliefs appear to impair health as they create a toxic environment, weaken our immune system, and increase stress hormones and blood pressure. In addition, they tend to increase depression and anxiety. Positive or healthy beliefs may increase our sense of well-being, instill hope, and provide meaning to our lives.

As we engage in our own spiritual and religious journey, understanding some basic ideas of other beliefs can be useful. The three major Western religions are Judaism, Christianity, and Islam. All three are monotheistic, meaning the followers believe in one supreme being who created and sustains the universe. The three major divisions in Christianity are Roman Catholicism, Eastern Orthodoxy, and Protestantism. Christianity is the largest religion in North America, but Islam is the fastest-growing religion in the

4. Jones, A., D. Cohen, B. Johnstone, et al. 2015. "Relationships Between Negative Spiritual Beliefs and Health Outcomes for Individuals with Heterogeneous Medical Conditions." *Journal of Spirituality in Mental Health* 17(2): 135–152.

United States and throughout the world. Of course, there are many different types of churches and beliefs within these divisions.

The major Eastern religions include Hinduism, Buddhism, Confucianism, Taoism and Shintoism. These religions are typically polytheistic, with a belief in more than one god. They often include a pantheon of gods or entities manifested in the forces and laws of the universe. Hinduism is one of the world's oldest religions and includes the concepts of karma and reincarnation.

A separate group of people is atheistic or agnostic. Atheism is the disbelief in the existence of a god or gods. Agnosticism holds that the existence of a god or gods is unknown and unknowable. Atheists and agnostics often hold the importance of human value and goodness or humanism, emphasizing common needs and a fulfilling life without traditional religion through experience and rational reasoning.

This book is not designed to provide details on various religions or beliefs but to offer an overview, to open a dialogue of understanding as to how different cultures or groups may have perceived the pandemic and reacted to it. Your view may follow that of your religious or spiritual group or diverge from it.

Other groups exhibit spiritual responses to natural events. Native American tribes often relate such beliefs, leaning toward harmony with nature, a cosmic identity, a sense of timelessness and predictability of nature. Their tribal rituals and ceremonies provide a code for ethical behavior and social organization. Their beliefs about health evolved from their religion. Health is harmony with oneself, including body, mind and spirit, harmony with others and harmony with one's surroundings or environment.

The Aborigines of Australia have similar beliefs. There is a kinship with the environment since they believe all objects are living and share the same soul and spirit. People, plants, animals, landforms and celestial bodies are interconnected. They believe that the universe began at the Dreamtime. They look to the power and ongoing relationship with their ancestor spirits. Many African belief systems share some similarities and have a strong belief in the role of their ancestors.

Every country and group of people in the world has a history of spiritual and religious beliefs. By learning more about other belief systems, we can better understand our beliefs and become more tolerant of others.

These two forces of spirituality and religion hold power to renew our hope, provide guidance, and prevent us from dissolving into despair. They provide values, moral codes, and a sense of peace, happiness, and contentment. They also offer the key to stepping into the future with a powerful weapon to withstand the tragedies and inequities of life.

With the many iterations of COVID-19, we may at times feel the need to renew our spirits, to reach out for support or affirmation. Our religious and spiritual institutions generally operate through the services performed through their clergy or leaders. These individuals may be called ministers, priests, rabbis, shamans, imams, or other titles, depending on the religion or belief system. They hold a position of authority within the organization. They may act as counselors to listen and advise following the tenets of their faith. Importantly, they can provide support, empathy, and compassion when tragedy strikes. When you need a support person, do not overlook your spiritual adviser.

As you examine your responses to COVID-19 and its aftermath, you may find that you have been impacted by significant anxiety or depression. Perhaps you felt overwhelmed by job loss, working from home, and the restriction of your life. Perhaps when the vaccines arrived, you felt a sense of relief or maybe even fear. When you turned to your beliefs, your "church" family, or your spiritual support system, perhaps you experienced even more confusion.

For some individuals, the problems relevant to therapy may include a crisis of faith, conversion to a new faith, life-threatening or terminal illness, or guilt and shame resulting from membership in a religious cult. For others, there could be religious conflicts in their relationships, disbeliefs in interpretations of scripture or religious doctrines, or a combination of psychotic disorders with religious content.

You may want to consider a professional counselor to help you examine some of your conflicts. These trained providers recognize and respect all spiritual and religious perspectives. They can modify their techniques to include their patients' spiritual and religious beliefs and set goals that fit with their patients' needs and beliefs. These professionals are not judgmental but can examine the role of an individual's beliefs in developing personal growth and development. Conversely, if the patient is experiencing a diagnosable mental health disorder, the therapist can integrate the management of those symptoms into the treatment program.

As you begin the process of bouncing back from the pandemic, consider the well-being of your body, mind, and spirit. Ask yourself, "What do I believe? What propels me forward to achieve beyond COVID-19?" As you examine these questions, take out your journal and jot down your immediate thoughts. Then, think back to your childhood and review your own experiences with belief systems. You might look at some of the following items.

What are your earliest memories of a belief or value system?
Did your family belong to a specific religion or belief? If so, what?
Did your beliefs change over the years? If so, how and why?
List six of your most important values. Where did they come from?
Do you have any conflicts with your own beliefs or with those of family or friends? If so, why? Have you found positive ways to manage those and not interfere with your relationships?

As you move through this self-analysis, you may discover that you have evolved over the years. The belief system of your parents may no longer fit with what you now believe. You may continue to evolve to a way of thinking and believing that fits who you are, which is part of the human development process. The key value of this exercise is to realize that your beliefs play a huge role in your interaction with other people, animals, nature, and the world in which we live. Our beliefs point us to purpose and gratitude for our existence. They provide us with reasons to continually renew ourselves. We all are works in progress.

Your success in reshaping your life begins as you review your responses to COVID-19 and engage in the process of rebalancing yourself through medical care, mental health treatment, support systems, and spiritual or religious beliefs. However, all your efforts can be for naught if you allow negative and dangerous attitudes and behaviors to take control of your life. Beware of thinking pitfalls that can prevent you from enjoying a peaceful and contented life.

9

Pitfalls to Progress

What were you doing in the spring of 2020? Those months brought a critical change in our lives as Americans. One day we were going about our daily routines. The next day some of us sat in front of our TVs, now aware of how quickly our lives, decisions, and fortunes could change. How we dealt with that and all the days following depended largely on our thinking processes. As discussed in Chapter 2, the brain believes the messages that we send it. How you managed your thinking during the pandemic may well determine how you have adjusted to life after COVID.

If you believed that the pandemic was awful, terrible, and unbearable, it's possible to continue that negative thinking after you have tossed the masks. If you told yourself that the lockdown was almost a vacation and you had a great time playing games with your family and enjoyed your hobbies, that, too, can follow you forward.

To readjust in the most successful manner after the restrictions on your life, it's very important to examine pitfalls, which can bring you down. These pitfalls can lead to continual negative thinking, infecting your life long after COVID has faded.

This chapter will examine several pitfalls, also known as thinking or distorted errors. All people have some thinking errors. Some errors are fairly harmless and easily ignored. Even the least difficult errors are often unrecognized until they are called to our attention. By reviewing your thinking process, you may be able to combat those hindering your progress to stability and contentment.

Take a few moments with each of the following pitfalls and ask yourself if you have ever experienced them. Are you experiencing them at this time? Consider ways to combat those thinking errors. In doing so, you may be able to enjoy even more contentment and stability after COVID.

The Blame Game

Who or what do you think is responsible for the COVID-19 outbreak? Is it a rat, a bird, maybe an insect? What about an enemy deliberately infecting our country? And after the outbreak itself, do you blame the government? Perhaps individuals who chose not to wear masks or social distance? Maybe you blame God.

Blame is a dangerous game. It removes the focus from self and taking responsibility for our actions in many cases. It fills our thoughts with negative concepts, even ideas of conspiracies and revenge. It prevents us from focusing on positive ways to manage our feelings and behaviors. Instead of examining how we can personally manage the crises, we can become overwhelmed by these thoughts.

When we are aware of our emotions, we can re-channel our thoughts by focusing on our issues. How will you manage with no income after losing your job thanks to COVID? But, more importantly, what were the positives? Perhaps you were able to spend more time on home projects or playing board games with your children. Now you can seek out a job that's more financially and emotionally rewarding. This process of reframing your thoughts is key to avoiding the pitfalls discussed here.

Black or White Thinking

This is also sometimes referred to as all or nothing, no gray areas. People are either good or bad. Did you ever find yourself thinking your fellow Americans are all either left or right, Democrats or Republicans, or conservative or liberal? To reframe this, look at your views. Some of your thinking may be quite conservative. Perhaps you feel conservative in how you elect to spend your money. You may consider yourself liberal in other areas, perhaps in equal rights or legalization of some drugs.

Recognizing that people and events are complex is a solid

foundation to avoid this pitfall. Stepping back and analyzing your black-and-white thinking is an essential part of making healthy and rational change.

Labeling

Labeling occurs when we refer to people as being "stupid," "dumb" or "ignorant" or when we label them based on race, religion or sexual orientation. We can also label social media, newspapers, and television networks as being "wrong," "slanted," or "right- or left-wing." We label both individuals and organizations with these and other terms.

What this labeling does is take away our objectivity. Instead of examining facts from many sides and reaching logical conclusions, we throw out meaningless and sometimes harmful words which can create serious consequences for others and yourself. It also deters us from recognizing the positive contributions and aspects of people and organizations. The need to reflect on oneself is usually ignored in favor of throwing stones.

"Musts" and "Shoulds"

Have you ever thought that it's not fair that you had to wear a mask? Did that violate your freedom? Maybe you told yourself, "It's not fair," referring to the pandemic itself or your loss of work hours and your inability to travel and visit family in another state.

I have a surprise for you. *Life is not fair!* It is full of injustices. It is full of natural disasters, the death of loved ones, dishonesty, war, and many other occurrences brought about by Mother Nature and by people themselves. People injure us physically and emotionally. They rob us, take our dignity, and lie to us.

When we use this thinking error, we believe that the world should be a certain way, that the conditions under which we live should ... you can fill in the blank. People should behave and believe in a specific way. I must be able to go to that store without any restrictions. There is a tendency for all of us to change our wishes into musts and absolutes. When the conditions around us do not meet our expectations, we can become angry, agitated. We may turn to social media to express our discontent. We might even get violent. We may indulge in the blame game as well as labeling.

"Musts" and "shoulds" interfere with rational thinking. Some events cannot be changed. All of our stomping and shouting will not make it different. Failing to accept this prevents us from moving our minds to a more peaceful and logical place.

Mind Reading

Did you ever think that your neighbor spurns you because your political views are different from his? Or perhaps you think that he believes that the world is doomed, that the pandemic is the introduction to the apocalypse or end of times. Maybe you think he is one of those tree-huggers and clings to a belief in global warming.

This pitfall is known as mind reading. We cannot see into the minds of other people. That neighbor may spurn you because your dog wakes him at 6:00 a.m. and he is fearful of bringing up the subject. Is the world going to end due to the pandemic? Probably not. If you were to review the various times that someone has declared the end of the world is coming, you might decide that he is wrong. Even the meteor strike over the Yucatan about 66 million years ago did not destroy the Earth.

Yes, COVID-19 is a huge inconvenience. But if we want to know what others are thinking, we can strike up a conversation with them. We can check the science and chances of human survival by researching the data. But ultimately, the best way of managing this pitfall is to focus on yourself. You can do this by setting up personal boundaries and avoiding worrying about others and the outcome of events you have no control over.

Denial and Minimization

COVID doesn't exist. Period. Total denial. Or you minimize it in some way. It's nothing more than the flu. Perhaps you or someone you know has stated and held some of these ideas. No matter how many reports you hear from the Centers for Disease Control or news organizations or podcasts, you refuse to believe that this infectious disease is anything more serious than allergies, a cold, or the flu.

The problem with flat-out denial is that you refuse to let other information in. If you hear something that contradicts your belief, you simply ignore it, push it aside, and insist that the information is wrong. Minimization is similar, but you allow in only what fits with your beliefs. Either way, you limit your brain to other possibilities and thereby block your reshaping possibilities.

Catastrophe

Do you view the past months as horrible, awful, unthinkable? Do you see them as unmanageable, horrific, and catastrophic? Your point of view probably affected the way you managed your behavior and life during these months. If you felt that it was the calamity to end all calamities, you may have become irritable and angry. Did you yell at your kids who were underfoot? Or holler about the schools and the governor closing them? This exaggerated reaction most probably contributed to your anxiety.

Of course, we felt frustrated and upset over the pandemic and the intrusions in our way of life. Such emotions were a normal response to the situation. However, negative feelings do not have to be catastrophic unless we allow them to be. Such pitfalls only hamper our journey to a new beginning.

Reframing the Pitfalls

Reframing was first mentioned in Chapter 2 as a method to recognize and examine a negative belief you have. Accept responsibility for it and then do a "mind switch." In other words, what is the opposite of that specific pitfall? What are other options or possibilities for revising my thinking? If you believe you have fallen into some of the ways of thinking listed above, what can you do about it?

Reframing is a cognitive technique often used in therapy to assist patients with identifying and then examining ways that their perceptions of events, ideas and emotions may be altered into a more positive point of view. However, reframing is a process that you can do by yourself. As with all personal change, recognition of the need for change is essential, along with acceptance. Beginning to trust yourself to make a safe and long-lasting renewal is also critical.

Beyond that, a variety of methods and tools exist to aid you in reframing. The following list is only a sample. You may be able to create your list based upon your specific pitfalls.

- Journaling. As mentioned earlier, journaling or jotting down your thoughts with all their distortions can aid you in facing what you have written—the words on the page or the screen. To view the letters formed before your eyes can create a determination to make that brain switch.
- Questioning yourself. Ask yourself questions such as "Is there another point of view?" "What are three positive things I've experienced from COVID?" "What would you say to your daughter who felt this way?"
- Looking back. Look back on ideas or views you have held in the past and altered as you've gained more information and experience. Make a list of them. Why did you change them? Perhaps you once thought tattoos were idiotic. Now you display the butterfly on your shoulder. Transfer that thinking to your negative pitfalls, those which can prevent you from reshaping your life.

Were you able to spot any personal pitfalls that you've experienced in the past, during the pandemic or since the restrictions have lessened? If so, you might make a list of the items and determine one way to alter your reaction in the future. Once more, turning to your journal to track your progress can provide a guide for positive change.

While distorted thinking can interfere with progress, one other pitfall may completely stop you in your tracks—addiction.

10

Addictive Behaviors

During the pandemic, some people turned to alcohol or other drugs for the first time, perhaps to manage their feelings or because they were bored. Others who were already addicted may have increased their use to dull their emotions further and combat their fears which ran the gamut.

Will all the toilet paper be gone by the time I get to the store? Does it even matter? Will I get sick and not be able to see the doctor? Some people who felt as if the threat of death were hanging over their heads might have given up and continued to use. By drinking, eating, or taking drugs, people could avoid the reality of their feelings surrounding the pandemic.

Still others, possibly even yourself, may find that the return to "normal" has created greater stress and anxiety. Now you have to interact with new faces at work and people hired while you were safely working at home. Now you have to trudge to the grocery store and brave the throngs of people clustered at the end of the aisles, happily engaged in idle gossip. You feel your heart pounding, and you just want to have your groceries delivered for the rest of your life. For you, grabbing a six-pack may provide a quick release from the fear that grips you. This reaction to the pandemic could lead to long-term use or addiction.

Whether you began using alcohol or drugs as a means of coping with the pandemic or recovery from it or you are a long-term addict, now is the time to break that cycle and establish sobriety and balance in your life. But how does one break addictive chains?

Addiction is a complicated and powerful entity. The very definition is dependence. Addicts often fail to complete obligations at work, home or school. They may continue to use even when they have recurrent social or legal problems. There is a tendency for the person to develop tolerance for his drug of choice or need more to reach the same effect as in the past. Sometimes people neglect their family and may have blackouts or flashbacks as a result of use. Even when an addict's family complains, the addiction may still take precedence. One example is a woman who describes her boyfriend's use of heroin and gives him an option: her or the drug. He chose the drug, and six months later, he was dead from an overdose.

As noted earlier, drug use can cause brain damage. To heal the injured brain is a challenging journey, a step-by-step process best guided by experts. A clean and sober support person or friend is essential. Engaging in treatment with a licensed addiction counselor or therapist can provide even more tools for a successful outcome.

Some people who exhibit long-term damage may benefit from a more intensive level of treatment. A trained therapist can test and evaluate the needs and make referrals as necessary. Available are four continuums of care: outpatient services; intensive outpatient or partial hospitalization, if needed; resident and in-patient programs, thirty-day and longer, depending on the patient's specific needs; and medically managed and integrated services.

Care may depend upon the type of drug used, the amount used, the date it was last used, the length of time it was used, and, of course, any past attempts of sobriety. Some people tend to separate alcohol from other drugs, but alcohol is a drug and is often considered the major substance contributing to personal and legal problems in our country.

Alcohol is socially accepted and legal. It can be purchased in almost any store in the country and at liquor stores, taverns, restaurants, and other locations. Alcohol, whether consumed as beer, cocktails or wine, affects virtually every organ in the body. The absorption rate varies depending on the gender and size of the user and the amount consumed in a certain time frame. Alcohol is responsible for decreased reaction time, as demonstrated in many scientific trials. Thus, accidents causing injury and death can result in criminal charges and financial ruin. Alcohol often plays a huge role in arguments and the ability to process emotions and contain behavior, which leads to physical abuse and even death.

A variety of treatment services may be necessary. Individualized therapy and group therapy are the two most frequently considered. Individuals are sometimes referred for treatment after they overdose or binge drink and engage in aggressive and hostile behavior, leading to an arrest. Some people may require a few days of withdrawal before treatment can be initiated. Inpatient treatment can last from two weeks to a year, depending upon the availability of services and the cost to the patient and whether insurance or payment options exist.

Many people with alcohol addiction engage in support groups to aid them as they struggle to remain clean and sober. The most well-known is Alcoholics Anonymous (AA), founded in 1935 by Bill W. and Dr. Bob working to overcome their drinking problems. They developed the Twelve Step program to aid in recovery from compulsive, out-of-control behaviors and restore manageability and order to one's life. The steps encourage honesty, humility, acceptance, courage, compassion, forgiveness, and self-discipline. They open doors to positive behavioral change, emotional well-being and spiritual growth.

There are alternatives to the Twelve Step program, including Self-Management and Recovery Training (SMART) and Rational Recovery (RR) and listings through the Substance Abuse and Mental Health Services Administration (SAMHSA). Many of these options include secular alternatives and emphasize internal control and medical options.

These self-help groups and programs can also aid individuals working to beat other drug and behavior addictions. This chapter is not designed to extensively cover all types and effects of drugs, but we will look at some other substances readily available to the public, including cannabis (marijuana), hallucinogens, inhalants, opioids, sedatives, stimulants, tobacco, and caffeine.

Marijuana or cannabis has gone from being the "reefer madness" drug to being recognized as legal for medical use in thirty-six states and four out of five territories and the District of Columbia. However, it remains illegal under the Controlled Substances Act of 1970 as classified under Schedule I or having a high potential for abuse and no accepted medical use. Legislation is currently underway, which may alter this soon.

The controversy surrounding marijuana continues. Concern

remains that marijuana contains the same carcinogens and cocarcinogens as tobacco, leading to lung and other diseases, legal problems, and addiction. Some people report that marijuana use helps with managing anxiety, stress, and depression. Others disagree, stating that its use is an excuse to get high. The research regarding medical use appears accurate, with cancer, multiple sclerosis, and seizure patients gaining relief from their conditions due to their use of marijuana.

The legal sale of medical and recreational marijuana has continued to grow, providing tax money for state and local projects. Yet, concern continues that greater frequency of use and higher levels of use results in lack of motivation, short-term memory loss, and impaired driving skills.

A major concern has been the use of **opioids** for pain relief following surgery. Opioids include heroin, a drug that depresses the brain and can suppress breathing. When patients can no longer obtain a prescription, they have been known to turn to street drugs such as heroin. Overdoses can occur and even lead to death. If it is used in time, Naloxone can save a life. The combination of medication and therapy can aid in overcoming this addiction.

Stimulants include cocaine and methamphetamines. These substances raise the level of dopamine in the brain and boost feelings of pleasure and happiness. However, they also produce negative side effects, such as headaches, strokes, breathing problems, withdrawal symptoms, and, like many addictive drugs, death. A major problem with both stimulants and opioids is that they are readily available from street dealers.

Tobacco use is considered the leading cause of preventable death in the United States; half a million people die each year due to smoking or exposure to secondhand smoke, according to the Centers for Disease Control and Prevention (CDC). Yet, people continue to use, even when presented with the facts.

Why? The reason is simple. Like many other substances, tobacco works on the pleasure center of the brain and provides a sense of relaxation and happiness. People often turn to cigarettes when they are anxious, worried, overwhelmed or "just need to relax."

It's not surprising that during COVID-19 some people opened a pack and then another to relieve their stress, and as the pandemic fades, some people will experience nervousness and fear at readjusting to the onslaught of people and myriad choices now offered. The good news is that with counseling, prescribed medication, and good nutrition, people can overcome nicotine addiction.

Caffeine is often overlooked when we talk about addictive drugs. Generally speaking, a cup of coffee or tea in the morning is not considered addictive. It is habitual for many. Yet, if a person drinks six pots of coffee a day and is nervous and jittery when he stops or is limited, that might be considered an addiction worthy of treatment.

Events in our personal lives and those on a larger scale, such as the pandemic, affect our senses, emotions, bodies, and relationships. In other words, they are inclusive, and as we struggle to manage our responses, we can benefit from honestly reviewing our journey. As we do so, please do not neglect the connections of your total well-being, including mental health. Most individuals who have addiction problems also have a coexisting mental health disorder. Again, such problems can best be diagnosed by a therapist and, in more severe cases, a psychiatrist who can provide a comprehensive evaluation or assessment.

Other Addictions

While this chapter has primarily focused on alcohol and drug abuse, addiction comes in many forms. Gambling, sex, pornography, the Internet, and food are several other examples. I like to think of addiction as any behavior or habit that occupies a large portion of one's thinking, intruding into daily life, robbing us of resources (such as money and time), taking us away from family and friends, intruding on our work and healthy activities. Therefore, almost anything can be an addiction, including our fantasies and our hobbies. Excess—that is the key.

Food: Adjusting after COVID means we have more choices to make. During the pandemic, you had fewer choices, staying at home, relying on the groceries available for delivery or in local stores. Now with restrictions eased, people must make more decisions. For some people, this has been an easy adjustment. But for others, possibly yourself, two dozen kinds of cereal, twenty types of coffee, and hundreds of drink choices line grocery store shelves; deciding which to purchase can produce anxiety. Faced with such decisions, some people find themselves more stressed, agitated or overwhelmed, which can lead to further fears and other addictive behaviors.

The pandemic meant that most of us were confined for an extended period of time primarily to our homes. What did you do inside? What activities aroused your interest? Watching TV, listening to music, playing video games—all enjoyable activities. But one activity that we all had to do if we were to survive was to *eat*. We either had to cook, get our food delivered (at least initially), and later eat out under certain restrictions. Preparing food in the home is and was vital.

During the pandemic, a major issue for some was inactivity which led to boredom. If you're not cautious, eating and food itself can lead to addiction. Whether you were working at home or just restricted in your activities, selecting healthy foods and maintaining a regular meal schedule might have been difficult. It might have been far too easy to rely on snacks and fast food. The chips or cookies were easy to reach after throwing a load of laundry in the washer or writing a work-related report.

For some individuals, the pandemic added additional pounds, slowly creeping in despite their best efforts. Now, with the passage of the initial pandemic fears, you may decide that it's time to cut back on the treats. A talk with your medical provider may be in order. A step on the scale and a review of your usual and ideal weight can be helpful. If you have gained a few pounds, perhaps only five or ten, the solution may be simple. Cutting back on carbs, soda and bread and walking around the block a couple of times a week may be the easy fix. However, if the gain has been significant, it may require a more substantial program. In any event, your primary medical provider should be consulted and relied on for appropriate and healthy solutions.

Internet Addiction

Perhaps you have always enjoyed the Internet. You can shop online, read books, and take that college class you always wanted to sign up for. The Internet gives you the ability to point and click and instantly find facts. You always wondered what happened to that little boy who played Beaver Cleaver. Now, you know.

This amazing electronic world serves us well. We can pay our bills online. We can price check that washing machine before we purchase it. We can see the Colorado Avalanche versus the Toronto Maple Leafs without leaving our recliner. We can share our pandemic frustrations on Facebook with all our friends.

With the arrival of COVID, suddenly we were confined to our homes. Initially, we could not go to work or shop at the local mall. We had plenty of free time to explore the Internet in all its forms. As a result, we may have spent more and more time pointing and clicking. Hours passed as Facebook and other sites took over our lives. Perhaps you even forgot to eat lunch.

As a result, you may have found yourself unable to ease up as the pandemic eased up. You managed to get your vaccines and return to work part-time, but you spent every available moment on the Internet. You're struggling now to best your opponents on *Call of Duty*. Regardless of your personality style or traits, perhaps it's time to examine your Internet habits. Have you developed an actual addiction?

Internet addiction is a growing concern in society. Known commonly as Compulsive Internet Use (CIU), it has been compared to other addictions but is not yet recognized officially as a disorder in the *Diagnostic and Statistical Manual of Mental Disorders* (*DSM-V*). Some reports suggest it affects up to 38 percent of the population.[1] Some evidence suggests that the effect on the brain is similar to that of drugs or alcohol. Other studies link Internet addiction to changes in the brain's prefrontal region and the release of dopamine to produce a pleasurable sensation. Some researchers believe that Internet addiction is a subset of media addiction, including television and radio and our cell phones.

How can you decide if you may be experiencing Internet addiction? The symptoms include many of the same symptoms of any addiction:

---

1. Gregory, Christine. 2018. "Internet Addiction Disorder—Signs, Symptoms, and Treatment." Psycom.net, February 14. Updated May 6, 2021.

Feelings of guilt: Have you ignored your family? Missed a ball game or two?

Dishonesty: Have you called in sick so you could finish that video game?

Inability to prioritize or keep schedules: Did you miss a dental exam, perhaps a parent-teacher conference?

Feelings of euphoria when using the computer: You feel good about yourself and your ability to navigate the Internet. You feel excited and can't wait to grab your coffee and hit the keyboard each morning.

No sense of time: You just looked up your favorite celebrity, and you are still moving between screens three hours later. You forgot to pick up the car from the garage.

Defensiveness: When your spouse criticizes your computer time, you jump back and say, "Well, I needed to check those prices on the kids' shoes." You make excuses.

Avoidance of work: Have you called into work so you could play video games or explore Facebook or your writer's group?

Any of these results might be a reason for concern. Addictive behavior triggers a release of dopamine, which promotes a sense of pleasure. However, it also can lead to an increase in mental health symptoms.

Fear: With easy access to the news, you may have experienced fear and confusion over COVID-19 and appropriate strategies of distancing, masking, or cleaning. Then as the pandemic appeared to ease, you may have felt relief. But as the hours pass and you hear the news reports, your fear level remains.

Anxiety: Anxiety is associated with fear, and your stress levels may have risen, even as you won that game.

Agitation: Feelings of nervousness and stress, especially when confronted by others over your extended computer use.

Loneliness: Your only friends are on Facebook. In reality, you have stopped interacting with your previous friends, even with the return to normal activities.

Depression: Are you experiencing feelings of being "down," especially linked to the guilt you feel about using the computer so excessively? As you read the news reports on your computer, you wonder if the pandemic is ever going to end. The conspiracy theories emerge, sinking your mood lower.

Mood swings: Along with depression, are you now feeling excited or manic, your moods fluctuating, when interacting online or when you can't get access?

Boredom with routine tasks: You have no sense of pleasure or completion when you must do your laundry or load the dishwasher. Instead, you are continually thinking of checking your e-mail and Facebook, wanting to reach that new level in *Warcraft*.

Just because you use the Internet frequently or watch many YouTube videos or shop online does not mean that you suffer from Internet addiction. The trouble comes when these activities begin to interfere with your daily life, just like any other addiction such as sex.

Sex Addiction

Often associated with Internet addiction, sex addiction can include many dysfunctions ranging from compulsive masturbation to uncontrollable infidelity to illegal behaviors, including exhibitionism and making or watching child pornography. Lumped together, these dysfunctions affect between 3 and 6 percent of the U.S. population.[2] There remains disagreement over whether sex addiction, also known as a compulsive sexual behavior disorder, is a treatable mental disorder.

The rationale for this disorder not being listed in the *DSM-5* is that it does not cause physical symptoms of withdrawal. Another concern is to not stigmatize the LGBTQ and transgender communities or others who engaged in behaviors considered outside "normal" standards.

However, just like other addictions, sex addiction can result in adverse consequences, such as destroyed relationships, impairment in other areas of your life such as work, self-care, and hobbies. Similar to gambling, shopping abuse, and substance abuse, sexual addiction, when rooted in a desire to escape emotional pain, can result in a cycle of increased mental health problems.

---

2. "15 Sex Addiction Statistics That Will Shock You." n.d. Addiction Headquarters. https://www.addictionhq.org/sex-addiction/sex-addiction-statistics/.

Gambling Addiction

Similar to other addicts, compulsive gamblers have a hard time admitting they have a problem. Gambling can include buying lottery tickets, betting on sports, and making wagers in casinos. The *DSM-5* does consider gambling addiction a disorder, unlike Internet and sex addiction.

Persons addicted to gambling will return to "try to get even" as soon as feasible and rely on others for money when they have financial problems created by their gambling. Gamblers also often feel stressed and unable to manage their emotions. They are often preoccupied with past gambling experiences.

Many problems are associated with gambling, including family violence. Tempers often flare when rent money is spent on gaming tables or lottery tickets. When your partner catches you lying, or you lose your job over missed work, arguments ensue, which can rapidly escalate to physical abuse.

Theft and other crimes are also associated with gambling. Stealing from your boss or parents for gambling funds is not uncommon, as is writing bad checks. Getting cash advances on credit cards or borrowing against future paychecks are all known to create more disruption in the lives of those who become addicted to gambling.

Gamblers can end up in prison when they reach the "big time." They borrow too much from people who charge enormous interest rates and are already associated with the criminal world. When I worked in a corrections facility, I met a man who committed a murder largely due to gambling debts he could not repay.

Did you find yourself engaged in any addictive behaviors during the pandemic? If so, does that mean you are doomed? Of course not. How do you know if you need more substantial help in overcoming the problems? Once more, turning to your diary or journal can provide a starting point. Write down dates, times, and amounts of the beverage or drug or amount of time spent engaged in gambling, Internet addiction, or any other behavior that you see as problematic. Keep this list. Review it. Note any patterns of use. Do you recall any triggers that might have led to the behavior? The trigger could be as simple as a fight with your significant other. It might be a song you heard that brought a flashback of a traumatic memory that led you to consume the entire gallon of chocolate ice cream. Other triggers include the following.

Change: Any type of change—a job or a death—can produce stress or depression. Even events that are positive, such as a newborn child or a vacation, can be triggers. In addition, external events may cause stress. The intrusion of COVID-19 into your life certainly produced various changes, including worksite change and, in some cases, resentment.

Stress: Stress, whether at work or at home, due to finances or legal problems or something else, creates anxiety and health problems. The bad stress can block our thinking so that we make lousy decisions and even engage in distorted thinking.

Thought changes, including denial: Stress can result in blaming others, distorting events, and telling yourself, "I can handle it." When you don't communicate your emotions to others, you can end up making poor choices.

Complacency: You begin to think you are "healed," you are now in remission, and there's no way that you will slip up. You stop attending AA meetings or reviewing the Twelve Steps.

Judgment lapse: You might throw caution aside. You begin nitpicking others, especially family members and those around you. You may reach for that bottle or syringe more easily.

Return to alcohol or drug use: Finally, as stress builds and judgment lapses, you begin rationalizing your use, saying, "It's okay. Just this one time."

Contributing Relapse Triggers

Whatever addiction you may have experienced—alcohol or other drugs, food, the Internet, or something else—you have not struggled alone. Avoiding relapse can be a challenge. Successful people recognize that the journey is the hardest work they have ever done. To be successful has meant that they avoided many temptations along the way. Do not

hang out with acquaintances and visit locations known as slippery places;
stop prescribed medication without your doctor's orders;

keep alcohol and drugs around the house;
isolate yourself or fail to use your support system;
feel overconfident that you do not need help;
avoid getting help when you feel stressed or depressed;
engage in any other obsessive behaviors like overeating, gambling, working all the time, or risky sexual practices; and
ignore relapse warning signs and triggers.

Once you have completed this self-examination, it's a great time to reach out, if needed, to a counselor or therapist. Perhaps your search may reveal that you don't have a significant problem, that you were only acting out in response to conditions of your life at the moment. Perhaps you never had a problem to start with. However, your behavior may still be worth a consultation. If further evaluation or treatment is necessary, you can then make that decision.

The idea of reshaping your life means that you can take these baby steps to counteract whatever behaviors irritate you and stand in the way of your progress. Only *you* can do that. In the next section, you will be able to examine another key component in reshaping your life: productivity in the form of work and reaching out to give your time and efforts to others.

11

Essential Purpose

"Hi-ho, hi-ho!" sang the dwarfs in *Snow White* as they marched to the mines to engage in their labors. The pleasant music coupled with the delightful animation gave youngsters like me the concept that work was enjoyable, pleasant, and productive.

Yet, for many Americans, work was short-changed during COVID. Were you one of those who lost your job? Or perhaps your hours were cut. You spent your nights wondering how you would pay for the electricity and put food on the table. Stress mounted. Depression rose to staggering heights. Hard to feel very "hi-ho" at such times.

For others who worked from home, the prospect of returning to an office or a cubicle and being back with co-workers may seem intolerable. You have adjusted to a new routine. Now you are asked to make another change. And change is difficult. While it can be positive, it also coincides with the unknown. What changes have been made while you were away? How are you going to be accepted back by others?

Regardless of your situation, a key step in moving to a healthy lifestyle and shrugging off the negative aspects of COVID is *work*. Yes, work does have negative aspects. We laugh at the comedy *Nine to Five,* but the reality is that the workplace can be toxic at times. With specific rules, requirements, dress codes in some instances, and impossible expectations by bosses, at times it may seem difficult to navigate.

Yet, we all need a paycheck. In today's world, little bartering takes place. Your dentist won't let you mow his lawn to fix that cavity. Many professions have codes of ethics that do not allow trade-offs, and licensed individuals can lose their licenses over violating this requirement. But to pay the rent, to put shoes on your child's feet and to put tacos on the table, money is a must. I won't even discuss the role of "magic money" like bitcoin and other usable exchanges.

Yes, we all need money. Work, however, represents much more than money. Work is fuel for our soul. Work keeps us healthy in body, mind, and spirit. It allows us to resolve our frustrations, to escape from some of the frustrations in our home life. At work, we meet new people and provide necessary services to others. We gain education and strength through managing tough problems, both for ourselves and others. At the end of the workday, we arrive home, exhausted, ready to pop a frozen dinner into the microwave, and yet, there is that feeling, that satisfaction that we have given the best of ourselves to our workplace that day.

There are no perfect jobs, but I wish there were, sort of. But there are also no perfect people. Our co-workers and our supervisors come to work with problems, with the humanness we all have. They do not always tell us their problems, so sometimes we may get a grumble in return for a "Good morning." We do not know if their mother is dying or if they are about to lose their home or if their son was just sentenced to prison. We need to remember to be gentle and kind with others.

What if you were unemployed because of a COVID-19 layoff? You may be so discouraged you feel that finding work will be impossible. Yet, you are still going to need to pay the rent or mortgage. You need food to survive. Yes, perhaps you have been getting help with the stimulus checks. Perhaps you have been eligible for food stamps or programs to aid with childcare or commodity distribution. If you are truly disabled or if you are elderly, you may get a monthly check. All of that assistance and help are marvelous.

But what if you are not eligible or no longer eligible for help with housing, food, and utilities? Somehow you will need to explore employment options. What previous jobs have you held? What are your skills, your hobbies and interests? Gather all of your personal information, including dates of employment and previous duties, and make a list of those individuals who have evidence of your work history.

The value of this is that you will be required to list this information on an application, especially with duties you had and achievements you accomplished, even if it was as simple as winning a monthly attendance award. For certain positions, you will need to complete a resume and attach a cover letter, often with a list of references. Completing these forms and applications can be overwhelming. In today's electronic age, you can find templates that are relatively easy to complete. You can locate examples of cover letters and various resumes with power words as well. There is a saying that "looking for a job is a job," meaning that it requires real work to locate that position that is waiting for you. The outcome of all this effort is that you will feel "hi-ho, hi-ho" about your eventual job and celebrate when you get that first paycheck.

I am a believer that all work is honorable. I have worked as a waitress. The work is hard, and the pay is lousy, even with tips. Clerking in a store with sometimes rude people is trying but honorable. Yet, it is important to remind ourselves that we are doing a valuable service for others when we work. They may not always show appreciation, but you should remind yourself that you are helping that customer, patient, or client, and, in turn, that action provides you with a sense of self-worth.

What if you are discouraged? Even in your zeal to find meaningful work, you recognize that your qualifications are limited. Many positions advertise for college degrees and years of experience. First of all, remember that not all jobs require college degrees. Unless you have a specific goal in mind, such as teaching, you may not need a bachelor's or master's degree and certainly not a doctorate. Some positions require only a high school diploma or GED certificate or an associate's or two-year college degree. Vocational programs, such as welding and mechanics, can lead to a well-paying and successful career. However, in today's world, all jobs require knowledge of the duties and tasks it involves and a willingness to work hard and interact well with other people.

Even when job descriptions may mention a degree, sometimes experience can be substituted. And what about that experience? Once more, that may vary, depending upon your previous work or your volunteer and activity history. Keep a list of past activities and your contributions to use for future career-seeking times.

How do you begin to find a job? First of all, you can begin by asking your friends and associates. Today, most people search online.

You can post on Facebook or a public marketplace. You should contact your local workforce center of the Department of Labor and Employment to obtain a list of all potential jobs in your area. You can register with all available job sites. One of the most effective ways to find a job is to simply *ask.* You can walk down a street in your town and ask if businesses are hiring. They may say "no" or direct you to apply online or hand you an application. You can knock on doors and ask if people need yard work. Of course, homeowners do need to use discretion in these cases.

I never forgot the story of a man who came to the United States with his family when he was seven years old. He spoke only Spanish. I met him years later when he was a successful detective with a major organization. He told me: "I have never been without a job since I was seven." As a child, he worked the onion fields with his parents and gradually gained better jobs, graduated high school, and went to higher education.

Most of us can't do that. Not today. But we can make looking for a job a job, devoting several hours a day to finding one. Recognize that you will find self-satisfaction with a job and feel better about yourself and the goals you are setting. And being able to take your family out to dinner once or twice a month without worrying that you won't be able to pay the gas bill—wow. What a great feeling and sense of achievement!

The Joy of Volunteering

What if you haven't been able to find work? What if you have next to nothing to put on a resume or application? You feel frustrated, hopeless. Everywhere you go, the employer says they want people with experience. How do you get that experience? Sometimes you get lucky, and someone will take a chance on you, and you garner that experience. But that doesn't happen often. I have discovered a wonderful way to get experience. Yes, it does cost something. It costs *time.*

Look for opportunities to volunteer. Volunteers give their time and energy to others, to causes, to community needs. Usually, individuals participate in these activities due to their sense of commitment and caring. Unfortunately, they don't get paid. Often, they don't realize that what they are doing is considered experience that can be valuable on job applications and resumes. As a result, they often fail to document the times, places, and types of work. Keeping a notebook on hand during your volunteer service will jar your memory when you sit down to fill out job inquiries and make your search much more productive.

Volunteer work is to be found all around us. Here are just a few examples.

- Picking up trash in the local park.
- Helping at the local animal shelter.
- Mowing your elderly neighbor's yard.
- Delivering groceries to a home-bound person.
- Helping build a fence for a needy individual.
- Giving a ride to someone with no vehicle.

Can you think of other ways to volunteer in your community? Again, keep track of your hours, but more importantly, the types of duties you perform so that you can transfer the information to a resume for the next time you apply for a position.

Perhaps you are still struggling with the experience issue. A third method for gathering information is looking at your interests and activities. Maybe you play sports or referee, or perhaps you donate handsewn articles or bake cakes for fundraisers. Again, keep a record of the event or activity, noting the times and dates and the skills you used to produce the product. What skills, such as lifting equipment, interacting with people, or keeping paper records, did you use? What about those video games you play? They require concentration and reaction time. Those abilities can be transferred to the required applications, whether completed on paper or online.

If you persist with this process, keeping good records of your volunteer work and your skills and activities, you will be successful, and that satisfying job will eventually come to you. Remember that even with the frustrations or problems that may occur on the job, a job is vital to growth and success in re-establishing stability in your life following COVID and its variants. When combined, work, volunteer opportunities, hobbies, and activities create a sense of purpose in our lives.

A central part of that purpose is knowing that we are essential and positively contributing to the world. Suppose you wake up in the morning with no desire to get out of bed after losing your job. Maybe you tell yourself, "I can't do anything right. My dad always said I was a loser. Guess he's right."

Maybe you recall dropping out of school and never going back for that degree. That reinforces what Dad said. When you make it to the breakfast table, your wife says, "You didn't take the trash out again. What's the matter with you?"

All of these negative messages circulate in your head. Over the years, as you seem to accumulate more of them, you come to believe them. Your self-esteem crumbles with every perceived criticism. Your core self, who you are, has been wounded and your basic thought processes damaged. Psychologist Albert Ellis, who developed a type of psychotherapy known as rational emotive therapy, identified several irrational ideas that link to self-dislike. They include:

1. I must absolutely be loved or approved of by everyone I find significant in my life.
2. I must be totally competent and adequate in everything I do to be worthwhile.
3. When people act obnoxiously or unfairly, I should blame them and see them as wicked, bad, or rotten.
4. I must view things as horrible, terrible or catastrophic *when* I am treated badly or rejected.
5. I have little ability to control or change events.
6. If something is dangerous or fearsome, I should be terribly concerned about it and dwell excessively on it, making myself anxious.
7. It is easier to avoid facing life difficulties than facing them.
8. Your past can continue to influence your life and decisions.[1]

As you review these concepts, note how each one contributes significantly to injuring your identity. Such ideas create concepts that we can't be happy unless we have money, love, and other people's

1. Binder, Carolyn Sue. 1995. *Albert Ellis: Dogmatic Christianity Detracts from and Disables Individual Growth and Development.* Thesis. California State University Dominquez Hills.

approval. We can't feel worthwhile unless we achieve specific goals or make certain advancements in our lives. If someone faults us or doesn't like us, that means that we are "bad." We can also get the idea that all work has to be hard, difficult, even miserable at times, that to enjoy it and the "hi-ho, hi-ho" idea is contrary to nature.

When we hold onto these ideas, we can begin to feel inadequate. The idea of "something's wrong with me" can invade our spirit and create a sense of defeat, of uselessness, of life having no purpose. The Islamic poet Rumi said: "When someone criticizes or disagrees with you, a small ant of hatred and antagonism is born in your heart. If you do not squash that ant at once, it might grow into a snake or even a dragon."

How can we defeat such beliefs within ourselves to achieve harmony and balance in our lives? Did you know that our minds have three states? There is the reasonable mind, the emotional mind, and the wise mind. The reasonable mind uses our intellect and makes plans and decisions based on fact. We use the emotional mind when feelings control our thoughts and behaviors, resulting in impulsive acts with little regard for their consequences. Finally, the wise mind recognizes feelings, respects them, and puts them in perspective. Then we can respond rationally. Can you recall an experience you've had when you used each state of mind? Which state proved more effective in decision-making?

Take a look at the list of irrational ideas I provided earlier. Now examine each one and counteract it. This is a good opportunity to write your reactions to these negative ideas in your journal. Ask yourself if you've ever experienced these feelings. If so, how do you use the positive side to rebuild your strengths and self-esteem?

Start by using affirmations. Affirmations are strong, positive statements you say as if something you want is already true, which may require practice. An example is "I will wake up in the morning feeling rested." Usually, the shorter and simpler the affirmation, the more effective it will be.

Creative visualization is another way to combat negative self-talk. This technique can be used with affirmations to help you create a clear image of something you want to happen. Use your imagination to focus on what you would like to happen in your life. For example, you might think, "I want to visit my mother when

COVID restrictions permit." When you picture this, imagine talking to your mother, seeing her, hearing her, smelling her perfume, and touching her hand.

Creative visualization can also include creating your own "happy place," also sometimes known as a "safe place." It can be an outside scene or a room no one else can enter unless invited. This process is also mentioned in other parts of this book, reminding us how powerful it can be in building our strengths.

Focus on your personal strengths. It can be easy to dismiss our strengths when we are under stress, whether the cause is personal, from natural events, or from a catastrophe like COVID. Now is a perfect time to remind yourself of just how successful you have been in overcoming other obstacles. Make a list of five things you do well. Look at all areas of your life: family, work, spiritual beliefs, hobbies, skills, and values.

This book will continue to discuss the importance of balance but take another look at your own life as you review the text. View it is a wheel divided into five segments. Draw the wheel and label each segment: social, physical, work/school, emotional, and spiritual (includes beliefs and religion). Take your finger and remove one segment. Oops, something else gets overloaded to compensate, which occurs when we get out of balance.

Of course, there are times when life gets out of balance. We lose our job or experience a medical disaster. At such times, we rely on the other strengths in our life, such as our spiritual and social supports, to aid us in managing those events.

Return once more to those who have been support people in your life, people who have been positive influences, have similar values, and give you a smile when you are feeling down. Turn to them with smiles and trust.

On the road to building self-esteem, perhaps nothing is more valuable than love. Nothing is more important than love to the process of bouncing back from COVID, personal loss and grief, and the daily frustrations humans routinely encounter in life.

What do you think of when you hear or use the word love? Love, of course, is a feeling, an experience. It's an attitude, a decision, and a skill that we cultivate. Love comes to us from our parents, significant people in our lives, nature, the divine. It also comes from self, from accepting who we are, body, mind, and spirit, with all our imperfections.

Love makes us feel like we exist and are important to others and to ourselves. If we do not accept love from and demonstrate our love to others, then we often fail to receive affection in return. Love is the foundation for growth and finding harmony in our lives.

Unconditional love does not mean accepting all behavior from our loved ones, including our children or parents, or from co-workers. But we still love.

I repeat this to my dogs on occasion: "I love you all to pieces, but I do not like your behavior!"

As you continue working on this activity, please look back at your progress. From the day you first received the COVID-19 shutdown announcement until this date, how have you been impacted? How have you changed? Hopefully, you've been journaling your thought processes, your medical, emotional and spiritual journal. As a result, you've reached a stage where you feel more positive and peaceful in your life.

At this point, you may believe your journey is over, but we are all works in progress. You are still on the path toward renewing yourself for the final phase of personal growth and development to establish harmony in your life.

12

Building on Your Strengths

You have arrived at a stronger state of mind after weathering the fears and craziness of the COVID-19 pandemic and its variants. You may feel like you are "back to normal" or that at least you can manage life better, making your own decisions, traveling, shopping, gathering with friends and relatives, and generally feeling more content with yourself and the world around you.

But have you really? Let's recap where you are at this time.

You might have discarded your masks if you wore them at all. But then you learned that variants of COVID are on the rise. Now, you are hesitant. Some establishments may still require masks. Those of you who used masks may have a varied collection, including super hero, rock star, sports team, or plain "hospital" style masks. Even if regulations change, hang onto them and keep some in pristine condition. In another twenty years, they may be collectibles and bring big bucks at an antique sale. Don't forget that your masks have a dual purpose. Do you experience allergies when working in the yard? Grab one of those forgotten masks. They aid in preventing many other illnesses, flu and the common cold, for example.

Enjoy your favorite restaurant without a mask—and with friends. You may still be asked to mask to enter, but you can remove the mask when at your table. Now you can gather to celebrate a birthday or holiday with no concern for distancing. Some of you may have lauded the "no eating out" mandate because you discovered that you saved a few hundred dollars this past year. The point is that now you can once more enjoy food with fewer health reservations unless your favorite restaurant invokes further restrictions due to COVID variants.

You may now be attending your favorite sporting events. The

stadiums may not be completely full, but you are looking forward to capacity stadiums very soon. Yeah! And your teams may have dropped the distancing and mask requirements. You can yell for the touchdown and consume your favorite hot dogs and drinks without having to yank the mask down. The same with concerts. This past year, you may have viewed concerts on your computer, and it was wonderful to be able to do that and pay a Stage It fee with a tip for your favorite artist. But now you can attend, even if you are in the very back of the auditorium. The atmosphere is worth it.

If you haven't yet, you soon should be able to shop in your favorite grocery store, mall or big box store without masks or distancing. If you've been having most of your groceries and products delivered, you can stop that extra charge. FedEx and UPS will have fewer stops as you ease up on your online orders.

Overall, it might seem as if you have come through the fire and are now able to resume all your normal activities without negative consequences. At least, that's what many of your friends and co-workers might say. Yet, you are still struggling at times. Is this safe with the variants out there? Uncertainty resumes, especially if you are an introvert.

Sure, you've made some progress. But you find yourself cringing at the crowds in the store and dreading that trip to the post office. Remember that you have been content with your quieter and more productive life. As a result, you may continue to experience fallout from the "return to normal" or the confusion over whether anything will ever be "normal" again.

Whatever your personality style or methods of managing, you have numerous tools to aid you in further developing your strengths. Now is a good time to review the previous writings in your journal. Examine the gains and losses of the past months. The pandemic brought with it some pluses and some minuses. Take a sheet of paper and make two columns. Label one side plus and the other minus. Examine each item with an open mind. Which irritated you the most or cost you the most in terms of time or money? Which ones provided peace or relaxation? Which ones gave you joy? Put emotional words next to each item. Do you see the fallout from any items, perhaps areas you still need to process, to examine more closely to create a more contented lifestyle?

Perhaps COVID delayed some of your goals. Your schooling was interrupted. You didn't get to graduate. Your quinceanera celebration was delayed. You lost your job. All of these interruptions produced a range of emotions such as frustration or anger or fear. You may be carrying the residue from the emotional effects. You may be struggling to right some of the problems that resulted.

Did you lose a loved one to COVID-19? Did you acquire COVID yourself and are you now suffering from long-term side effects? These events may have traumatized you in ways you never realized. You may experience sleepless nights and feel jittery and easily irritated. Others report ongoing memory problems. Yes, we have all been brain damaged by COVID in some manner. You may have recovered well with fewer after-effects, while other people may report a longer, more difficult recovery.

Now, do the same exercise with life after COVID with variants present. List the pros and cons, the advantages and the disadvantages. As you move through this process, focus on your strengths. Often it is easier to ruminate on failures and negative decisions and outcomes in life. When you focus on your strengths, you can build on a solid foundation. However, this requires that you begin with a self-analysis to recognize and be aware of your strengths and build on them. The following checklist may be helpful as you examine your personal qualities. Feel free to number them from one to ten, one being the lowest strength and ten the best.

Family: Of course, family includes your parents, siblings, spouse, children, and significant others. However, the family can also be your community, your tribe, and any others who are essential and supportive in your life. If family is a high priority in your life, you will want to keep those individuals close to you. You will acknowledge any differences in opinions or beliefs and accept that it's okay to think differently and still love and engage with your family.

Resilience: Resilience is the ability to spring back when life events, such as COVID, derail you. If you have recovered from being sexually assaulted or neglected as a child, will you ever totally forget that? Of course not. But you have learned to manage your life beyond the event. Resilience includes springing back from your own poor choices that have created detours in your life. Did you sell illegal drugs at one time? Did you cheat on your spouse? Resilience also means that you have taken responsibility for past bad choices and are now successfully managing your life.

Faith: Faith includes your religious or spiritual beliefs and using them to manage negative emotions and events. Whatever your religion or foundation, using the power of your faith can lift you when life gets rough. People we love die; we lose our home to a flood; we are diagnosed with a fatal disease. Prayer or meditation can sustain us in those moments until we can stabilize ourselves.

Support systems: As previously noted, this includes family, friends and others who provide strength when you experience difficulties. Phone calls, texts, cards and emails can maintain those systems. Have you ever lost a friend because they moved a distance from you? With today's electronic communications, we should not allow that to happen. We need all the love and support we can get.

Communication: Your ability to listen, speak positively, observe, use body language to aid in being accurately understood and truly "hearing" what others are saying are all critical factors in positive communication. Without good skills, relationships can flounder, and conflicts spread like viruses, even infecting those we love.

Openness: Allow yourself to be open to learning new skills and facts and to be understanding of other points of view. When you close yourself off to accessing information, you can't acquire new knowledge. As a result, you might miss an opportunity for a new friendship, career, or activity.

Moral codes: How do you determine your decisions when in doubt? We often rely upon our beliefs or the rules and guidelines that are considered appropriate in our society. We refer to these as moral dilemmas or choices. Do we keep the lost wallet or attempt to return it? Do we partake of drugs with our friends or decline? Moral codes may be written like the Ten Commandments or unspoken agreements or pacts. They largely depend upon our cultural concepts, including generational factors, historic events, orientations, and beliefs. They include our thoughts, actions, and behaviors.

Values: Values include moral codes, as cited above—good versus bad, wrong versus right—but they also include such things as honesty, care, loyalty, kindness, trustworthiness, humility, and dedication. These values comprise your strengths. They are a measure of your character and who you are. Values are reflected in your day-to-day interaction with others. How do you address the people you meet at work? How do you respond to their remarks? The list of values could go on at length. You may want to add others, especially those that play a significant role in your life.

Work: How you view your contribution to your job or career indicates much about your values. How dedicated are you, not just to the job, but to helping and assisting your co-workers and customers? Work often interacts with values. Is it okay to steal copy paper from work? They will never miss one ream. Is it okay to leave ten minutes early or spend an extra thirty minutes over the coffee pot? How important is customer service to you? Do you feel pleased when a customer says, "thank you"? At the end of the day, are you satisfied with your contribution? How we treat our work is an indication of how we feel about ourselves.

Skills: Take a close look at your abilities to perform tasks. Are you good with your hands? Woodworking? Repairing leaks? Gardening? Fixing motors? Computers? All valuable assets, perhaps even a great addition if you are job hunting. They also provide excellent diversionary hobbies and activities when you feel stressed or "down" by taking your mind off negative thoughts or behaviors.

Hobbies: While hobbies may seem like ways to pass the time, they demonstrate your ability to focus and concentrate. They can also lap over into skills and lead to occupational assets. Your hobbies can range from playing video games to crocheting. The list is endless. Just like skills, hobbies offer diversion when we feel overwhelmed or anxious.

As you review this list and your scores, you may find other strengths that are not listed. Please add them and ask yourself why these are important to you. In fact, with each item listed, consider taking inventory. Why are they important in your life? In what way? Also, if you scored low on some, you may consider further developing those strengths.

Perhaps you didn't consider some of these items as personal strengths, but the important part of this process is acknowledging that you possess many outward and inner strengths. Using your strengths allows you to view the pandemic experience as a time when you can accept yourself and experience growth. Regardless of your personality and unique traits, you can now move to a more positive and contented self.

Continue to build on these strengths if you experience fallout from the pandemic and other personal trials. You can establish a new comfort zone in your life because of your positive qualities. However, do not allow yourself to be pushed forward by others. Use your strengths to move forward at your own pace. Don't be overly concerned about what others are telling you to do. You may adjust more quickly in some areas, with a calm sense of security and progress. In others, you may want to hold back and take baby steps toward personal renewal.

Take an inventory of your emotions and responses to your early reactions to COVID. Open your journal and write down what your thoughts were. Did you leave work that day, thinking you'd return in a week or so? One year later, you were still working at home. Did you have to learn new skills to manage Zoom and other types of programs to work with your customers or patients? How did that affect your relationships? Examining these early feelings and accepting them will aid you in moving forward.

Put your journal to work examining your current goals and feelings about reintegrating into your "normal" lifestyle, implementing positive changes in your after-COVID life. Again, disregard what others are doing. They may be driving ninety miles an hour, but you do not feel safe at that speed. You are perfectly content to stick to the sixty-five-miles per hour speed limit or maybe a shade under.

Did you feel safe removing your mask in stores and at events when the "all clear" was announced? The restriction may have continued to apply at some stores and companies. And just when you thought you had adjusted to a new comfort zone, you learned that COVID was not over. Instead, variants of the virus emerged, creating confusion. Did you return to masking? Did you still need to maintain six feet or three feet distance when interacting with others? Or maybe you were comfortable shaking hands and hugging. These have been your choices, not the decisions of others.

I suggest you review valid medical data, current CDC data and rely on community and business protocols as you journey toward reshaping your life even now with threats of COVID variants and other future pandemic possibilities. Be sure to use your safety valves, those friends and family who are supportive, and your medical and mental health and spiritual and religious guides.

To aid you in your success, I have compiled the following initial steps, including some exercises and suggestions for avoiding the pitfalls of blaming others, the government, God, or yourself. Remember, the blame game can take you to a reactive and negative position and foil your work on reshaping yourself.

Step 1: Turn Off the TV and Social Media

What is your favorite TV show? Do you binge some series? Have you ever dreamed about some of the characters? Do you need to watch every news broadcast? Perhaps you prefer one network over another. Left, right, conservative, liberal?

What about social media? Do you browse Facebook more than two hours a day, tweet your opinions for the world to see, listen to podcasts daily? Is it difficult to turn your phone off for six hours?

To regain a foothold in the "real world," to interact with others and focus on nature, work, or rekindling relationships, you can speed up the process by turning off your devices. Almost no one would like to go back to the 1930s when our only form of information was radio and newspapers. Today we all have become so addicted to our devices that we feel lost without them. How often have you seen people sitting in a restaurant together, texting on their phones with no verbal conversation between them?

One key to reclaiming ourselves is peace and quiet. Scripture states, "peace be still." There is wisdom in those words.

Turn the TV and phone off for *two hours* for your first free day.

Do you have to do this every day? No, but try it two to three times a week. Use that time for walking, meditation, playing with your kids, communicating with others. You may be amazed at the difference in how you feel emotionally and physically.

Step 2: Have Fun!

What do you like to do for fun? List three items that you enjoyed while you were stuck at home due to COVID. Hobbies and activities create a sense of achievement within our spirit. Once we have successfully participated in an event or completed a project, we can feel a sense of accomplishment, a satisfaction that uplifts our self-esteem.

Sometimes I greet patients who tell me that they have no hobbies, no outside interests. One of my first suggestions is to develop an interest in something new or perhaps something they once found absorbing but somehow lost along with life's interruptions. When we do not have outside interests or activities, several negative outcomes can result.

One side effect is boredom. Nothing to do. Nothing seems interesting. You stare at the TV. Blah, that, too, is boring. Boring. So boring. Soon you may begin to feel depressed, frustrated, angry, unable to find any challenge in household tasks. If you get bored enough, you may reach out for some way to lift your mood. Unfortunately, some people turn to drugs or alcohol. As noted previously, some people may overeat and snack throughout the day.

You binge watch television or spend hours locked into social media. Both can be productive, offering a positive distraction from our stressors, but addiction to them creates less interest in successfully managing your issues, setting personal goals, and engaging in a healthy lifestyle.

Perhaps you already have several hobbies and only need to consider how they can benefit your emotional well-being or be used to help others. Some hobbies can be turned into careers. For example, someone who enjoys sewing may become a designer. Those who enjoy yard work might become landscapers. Those who are fascinated by computers, with more education and experience, might become software engineers or have a business serving home computer users who run into problems.

You may now be asking yourself "What about me? What hobby could I learn or develop to help me recuperate since COVID-19 no longer presents a distinct threat?" The possibilities are endless and depend upon your personality, interests and past influences. The following suggestions are offered only as a guide.

- **Do yard work**. Planting, watering, mowing, and harvesting provide a method of tuning yourself into the wonders of nature. If you do not have a yard, you can bring a plant into your home or grow a window box of herbs. But anytime you have a chance, take the yardwork outside, where you can smell nature, hear the cry of the birds, and see the beauty of the grass and plants, which is a form of mindfulness all by itself and an awesome hobby that also recirculates oxygen back into the earth.

Today walk outside and smell the world, look around, and take five deep breaths.

- **Read**. A ninety-year-old man once said to me that his greatest regret in life would be if a day came when he could not learn one new thing. I never forgot his statement. We are indeed fortunate to have the sense of sight. Being able to read and understand language opens the mind. Options exist for those who are vision impaired. Braille is an awesome asset and newer electronic devices open the joy of reading to many others.

  I vividly recall meeting a child coming from the library who explained her attraction to books. She said, "Don't you know that you can learn anything from books, or you can travel anywhere you want to go?" A very wise remark from a six-year-old girl. Books do exactly that. We can learn and study information, but books don't just provide education. They contain a huge variety of entertainment genres. We can enjoy romance, science fiction, action, drama, poetry or any other topics that interest us. Taking an hour from a day to read is perhaps one of the best relaxation tools easily available. Some people prefer electronic books, while others, like me, enjoy the smell and feel of "real" paper books. Either way works.

  Read at least five pages in any book of your choice today.

- **Walk or dance**. Being homebound for many months never meant that you couldn't go for a walk using distance regulations. Following the pandemic, it is even more important to continue exercise, and walking is considered one of the best, both for weight control and cardiac health. If you aren't able to walk outside, you can walk around the house. If you have physical limitations, you can walk in place or dance. Try standing and leaning against a chair as you comfortably walk in place. If this is difficult, you can sit in a chair, place your feet flat and lift them up and down at an easy pace, or you may shift them sideways on the floor.

Another name for these activities is *exercise.* Your body needs activity, and your mind will further absorb the magic of movement. However, do not engage in any physical activity if you have medical conditions that would prohibit it. Consult with your medical provider first.

If you are physically able, walk or dance today for at least ten minutes.

- **Do crafts**. Crafts can be combined with art in that both are constructed by humans and provide a sense of achievement and wonder in our lives. You can choose to expand a current craft or learn a new one. Instructions are easily available through books and the Internet to learn almost any activity you might like to explore. Some of the crafts you might explore are knitting, crocheting, creating fishing lures, woodworking, macramé, sewing, or quilting. Perhaps you can think of others. The list of crafts is endless.

  List one new hobby or activity you would like to pursue and your plan for achieving the knowledge to enjoy it.

- **Take up art**. Art encompasses a wide variety of interests and activities. Typically, it is considered to be the creation of beautiful or thought-provoking works. Art creation is also considered therapeutic because it adds to one's self-esteem and sense of accomplishment and provides distractions from painful life events. Some subjects might include painting, tattooing, photography, sculpting, ceramics, and creating objects from other crafts, such as sewing, macramé, crocheting—the list is endless. Many of the areas overlap with others. Have you ever tried to draw a picture of your family? How about painting a picture? You do not have to be a professional artist. The joy of art is in self-satisfaction, in being able to lose yourself in the project. In other words, reducing stress, giving in to the relaxed and creative spirit. If you want to learn basic types of painting or drawing in perspective, you can find classes and instructions on the Internet.

Art also includes appreciation. You can educate yourself on the various ages and styles, methods, current trends, and local artists. You can view famous paintings and sculptures in person or on the Internet. I had the wonder of visiting the Louvre and viewing the *Mona Lisa* in person, an experience I shall never forget. You can view and even be a critic in the same manner. You can even attempt to copy some of the lines, designs and styles of famous artists.

More recently, I discovered paint by number. You can purchase kits in which you can paint the *Mona Lisa* or *The Last Supper*. This hobby brought great joy to my father during the last years of his life, and my greatest pleasure is that I have several of his paintings now in my possession. You can download applications for your phone and computer. You can then paint the numbers and save your prize paintings.

Art, music, and literature, considered by philosophers, sociologists, and, yes, even therapists, are key to the development of the human spirit and the mind. They appear to be essential to humanity. Evidence of art exists on the walls of caves and tombs through layers of Earth's history.

Draw a picture of your family as you recall them from childhood.

- **Play board games and cards**. Do you enjoy board games? List two favorites. Today the focus appears to be on video games, with people playing on the computer, the phone, or a gaming system. There is nothing wrong with using electronic devices, which can act as detractions from our stresses. However, sitting down with our family and friends to an old-fashioned board game can cement relationships. Sitting together, we can communicate openly, face to face, joke, and share drinks and snacks. We can learn new strategies, skills, and rules. Numerous games exist to whet the appetite of people of all ages, including checkers, Chinese checkers, Scrabble, Monopoly, Clue, chess (for those brainiacs), dominos and many others. Among card games, you can revert to Old Maid and Authors and work up to gin rummy, bridge, poker, and Pitch. Of course, there is always solitaire, and there are 540 versions of solitaire.

Pull out a board game you enjoy and play it with a family member or friend this week.

- **Do puzzles.** Puzzles are another way to develop your mental strength. They aid us in keeping our brains active, provide outlets for boredom, and act as a diversionary tactic when life stressors invade our thoughts. Puzzles are a form of games. They teach strategy and often are done as a pleasant pastime. They also act as a stress reducer. Those who study keeping our brains healthy recommend puzzles. What puzzles might interest you? Try crosswords. They come in all forms, easy, moderate, complicated. Word finds are another enjoyable brain game. Sudoku involves numbers but requires no math ability. Numerous puzzles, including those 1,000-piece picture puzzles, can take many hours to complete. And then there are those 3-D monsters to assemble. Go on an exploration and find one that works for you.

  Select one type of puzzle for yourself, complete it and describe how it helps your self-management skills.

Step 3: Breathe

As you read through this book, have you ever wondered why I continue to emphasize the importance of breathing? After all, aren't you breathing even as you read these words? If you are alive and functioning reasonably well, you are breathing. What is the point of repeating this exercise?

The type of breathing I encourage is often known as belly breathing or deep expansive breathing. The process is simple and very helpful when dealing with stress or anxiety. When I feel nervous, angry, or upset, I recognize that my anxiety ogre is at work. I accept that I am feeling this emotion. Then I visualize a stop sign.

This stop sign looks just like the one you might find on a street corner in your town. Visualize this image in your mind. It is giving you a direct order. Stop! Stop! Sit down. Sit in a sturdy chair, place your feet evenly spaced on the floor. Then, take a deep, expansive breath, way down into your diaphragm, hold it for a second or two, and then exhale, letting it out through your mouth. Continue with this, relaxing your shoulders, arms, and chest several times until you feel your mind relaxing also. You are clearing your mind, at least temporarily, of any anxiety or stress. More importantly, you are giving your spirit the gift of peace.

With the body scan exercise described below, this exercise can aid you in enjoying productive sleep. We reviewed the sleep issue in the medical chapter, as the importance of having a consistent sleep routine cannot be over-emphasized. I encourage you to take inventory at this time. Is it difficult, almost impossible, for you to fall asleep? Does your mind continue to jump from scene to scene like some silent movie? Are you up, down, and all around?

If this is your nightly routine, I encourage you to adopt a body scan program. Situate yourself in a comfortable sleeping position, lie still, take a belly breath. Now begin with your face. Tighten the muscles, make an ugly, scrunchy face, hold it for a second, and slowly let go, relax, breathe. Now, tighten your neck muscles in the same manner, hold, and slowly let go, relax, breathe. Move to your shoulders, tighten, hold, slowly let go, relax, and take a deep breath. Move to your arms, using the same process. Make a hard fist with your hands, tighten, hold, let go, relax, take a deep breath. Next, do the same thing for your chest, stomach, and go on to the hips, legs, feet and toes.

Try this process many times over for several subsequent nights or sleep times. It doesn't take that long, and you may find as you progress with this routine, you end up asleep before you have gotten all the way down to your toes! I encourage you not to give up. Be patient with yourself.

By continuing with your deep breathing exercises and other relaxation tools, you may discover that your anxiety, stress, and, yes, depression are more manageable. You will begin to recognize the body signs and find your stop sign quickly.

As you read this right now, **visualize the stop sign and sit down. Do the breathing exercise at least twice.**

Step 4: Travel

Have you ever thought that you'd love to go to Ireland? Maybe Australia? But then you are realistic. You don't have the money.

Maybe you can't travel to another country—at least not now. You are stuck where you are, in your town or city, your part of the earth, and what is the point anyway?

Travel allows you to move outside yourself to enjoy the scenery outside of your usual location. You can hear different voices, at least emotionally. Perhaps you can taste other cuisines, even if you just drive to another neighborhood. You can touch different trees and see different flowers and animals. In other words, travel aids you in expanding your senses. More importantly, it revives our minds and alters our brains in pleasant and exciting ways.

So, you can't go to Europe. But you can turn on Rick Steves' travel shows on PBS and vicariously enjoy the sights, sounds, music, and food. You can easily locate other travel shows or television movies and films featuring a location you hunger to visit. You can read a book set in or about those locations and perhaps view breathtaking photos of your dream vacation. Using your imagination, you can travel to outer space! Currently, I am enthralled by Australia, so I am watching many films which have led me to research more of the history and culture of the country.

While traveling to another country or across our own country may be impossible at this time in your life, it is emotionally rewarding to travel beyond your doorstep. As humans, we need to connect with other places and people. One wonderful and simple way to get the same benefit is to drive or walk to another neighborhood. Go across town and examine the homes, the buildings, the people as they walk about. Perhaps you can drive to a neighboring town or city. Check out the convenience stores and the diners.

The purpose of this exercise is to move outside of yourself. View other people, their way of life, their surroundings and environment, and examine the diversity of humanness. This can lift our spirits, reframe our depressed thoughts and feelings. Keep in mind that travel also includes walking, as we earlier reviewed.

Select a travel mode today, such as walking or driving. During the next week, set aside one afternoon or perhaps one hour to spend reflecting on the trip, using all your senses.

Step 5: Learn

During the pandemic, most of us were continuously getting new information. Some of that occurred in the form of facts about COVID-19—the symptoms, its prevalence in your community, and when and where you could get a vaccine. We absorbed some of this information. Other information did not seem relevant, so you may have ignored it at the time.

There's a saying that wise people learn and make changes accordingly. Many of us did exactly that during the pandemic.

Life is a process of learning. We often must learn to operate our upgraded phones or our computers and related software. We must learn new ways of performing old activities as simple as making bank deposits or operating the GPS on our car. Learning is brain food to nourish our mental health.

We can enrich our minds with new information and activities in a multitude of ways. One is simply to read a book. You can visit the local library or read online, where a wealth of information exists. YouTube offers demonstrations of activities from cooking to crocheting to changing your car's battery. The list is inexhaustible. Regardless of the format, the opportunity to learn and develop new skills boosts our energy and self-esteem.

Another method to learn information and skills is by enrolling in classes through your local college or library and online classes through various schools or organizations. Again, the knowledge available today is limitless.

Using your ability to learn new and valuable information is an asset that can break the curse of boredom, offer hours of productivity, perhaps lead to a new career, or generate a greater sense of self-worth. Learning contributes to a more positive mental health outlook, lessening the focus on our daily stressors and dilemmas.

Find a recipe for banana bread from scratch. Be able to describe the steps and, if you like, bake and enjoy it with your family or friends.

As you examine the various exercises described here, you may have noted some challenges along the way. You felt more comfortable with some of the activities than others. Build on those that work for you. Remember that through this process, you may have discovered that you could rely upon your inner strengths to complete the assignments. Your strengths aided you in determining your responses to COVID-19 and its variants.

But where do you go from examining your positive assets to facing the challenges and confusion of a "new normal" environment? If you are struggling with change, whether you perceive it as overwhelming or freeing, you may be able to build further insight by a review of routines and rituals in your daily activities.

13

Routine and Rituals

Routine provides a solid foundation for establishing new goals and parameters in your life. The very word *routine* can sound boring and repetitive, but that is deceptive. What it implies is a sequence of events that are familiar, stable. During the pandemic, your routine may have been disrupted significantly. Perhaps you began working out of your home and enjoyed it. Still, it upset your former pattern of dressing for work, traveling to work and returning home day after day. You missed your colleagues and now your children are home-schooled, a new parental experience for many. Routine medical and dental exams were canceled. As a result, the days may have seemed unsettling and boring. Those who had few hobbies may have resorted to television to occupy their days.

Whether you viewed the pandemic as a vacation from or as a disruption to your life, it affected you. There is no "right" or "wrong," but you have had to reframe your thinking process. Routines represent stability. From the time we get up in the morning until we go to bed at night, routine acknowledges the dependability in our lives. It signifies safety and removes uncertainty. Routine helps us diminish our fears. We know what to expect.

One benefit of routine is better sleep patterns, which contribute to keeping you alert, focused and energetic. Routines can improve your mental health by reducing stress. In addition, routines can result in improved physical health. Each routine day represents how we perceive our lives, full of satisfaction, jobs done with care, our families provided for, our dogs have bones, our checkbooks are balanced, and all is right with our world. When we float through our days with no stability and no purpose, we experience the opposite—increased stress, disturbed sleep and eating patterns, and aggravated medical issues. Boredom sets in, and idleness accentuates depression.

Routine keeps us in check. As we manage and hold dear those safe days, the routine provides us with a sense of what is "normal." We then gather strength to endure when storms rage and to reclaim a sense of normalcy. Routine reinstitutes balance in our lives, something we need to survive through dark days.

Routine provides several other positive benefits, as you can get things done more readily, such as taking that morning walk or swallowing those prescribed morning medications. As you create habits, you are less likely to leave your car keys in various places throughout the house, increasing your anxiety and frustration. You are also less likely to forget things, such as those morning medications.

You also can teach others. For example, teachers use lesson plans. Your planned routines often are viewed and imitated by others, including your children. With your schedule in place, specifically your morning schedule, you are more likely to arrive on time for work.

College professor Dan Erickson examines these benefits and points out the downside of routine.[1] He notes that if you have a strict schedule, you can resist change. You might turn down an invitation to a concert with a friend for fear of breaking out of your normal routine. Your fear of breaking out of your comfort zone might keep you locked away from many things you might otherwise enjoy in life.

Routine can result in a lack of creativity. Too strict a structure can keep you from being open and creative. We all need to shake things up now and then so that we aren't bored or boring. The key is to find a middle ground, a place that works for you. Each person is different. We do need routine, but we also need to avoid regimentation. We need to break out of our comfort zone from time to time.

Routines and rituals are especially meaningful in the total development of children. Research indicates that young children are

---

1. Erickson, Dan. n.d. "Routine: The Pros and Cons of the Same Old Thing." https://www.hipdiggs.com/routine. Accessed September 27, 2021.

keenly aware of the daily, weekly and annual rhythms of family life and are eager to be involved as central players.[2] Family rituals involve communication with symbolic meaning and help establish variations in relationship satisfaction and socio-emotional functioning. For example, exposing children to the routine of dinnertime aids them with developing language and socially accepted behavior. In addition, routines also aid in the development of academic skills, establishing a time, place, and attitude for the family to engage in activities such as joint book reading.

A vital part of routine may include individual and family rituals. Rituals develop around traditions, such as family reunions, prayer before meals, attending religious services, or quiet times. People frequently are not aware that rituals are a significant part of their existence. They may have faithfully continued them as part of their family heritage. For example, their parents brought them up with a specific religious or spiritual belief, which they continued in their family. As a result, they attend weekly religious ceremonies. In other cultures, they might visit and meditate at a site that holds significant meaning for their ancestors.

Rituals provide emotional benefits. They may reduce anxiety, boost confidence, alleviate grief, or enable one to perform well in competition. While we sometimes wonder about the effectiveness of rituals, some research indicates that the symbolic behaviors we perform before, during and after a meaningful event are surprisingly useful and more rational than they appear.

For example, basketball superstar Michael Jordan wore his North Carolina shorts underneath his Chicago Bulls shorts in every game. Research in sports psychology indicates that these pre-performance routines can improve attention and increase emotional stability and confidence.[3]

The ritual of baptism requires participation, whether the person being baptized is an adult or a child. In the case of a child, the parents select one or two godparents. The godparents have a responsibility

---

2. Spagnola, Mary, and Barbara H. Fiese. 2007. "Family Routines and Rituals: A Context for Development in the Lives of Young Children." *Infants & Young Children* 20(4): 284–299. https://journals.lww.com/lycjournal/Fulltext/2007/10000/family-routines. Accessed September 28, 2021.

3. Gino, Francesca, and Michael I. Norton. 2013. "Why Rituals Work." *Scientific American*, 14 May. https://www.scientificamerican.com/article/why-rituals-work.

to serve as a guide for their godchildren throughout their life, in all aspects of their life, which brings the parents a sense of comfort, reducing uncertainty regarding their child's future, alleviating fears and anxiety, and elevating their faith.

An example of a Christian ritual going back to about the 11th or 12th century is the recitation of the rosary. Primarily associated with the Catholic church, the rosary is a series of beads, a crucifix and a medal. Other religions also use prayer beads and rituals to aid in prayer and meditation. As users count the beads, they recite specific prayers. The rosary helps them focus and clear their mind and meditate more effectively. Other religions, such as Buddhism, Hinduism, and Islam, also use prayer beads.

These rituals activate a sense of control and reduce fear and anxiety. Typically, they include activities such as preparation. The result of many rituals is that those participating experience a renewal of their faith, a sense of peace and commitment.

Rituals are present in aspects of all societies, including worship, rites of passage, coronations, and inaugurations. Even daily activities such as handshaking, which we bypassed during COVID, and eating mark our accepted and expected rituals. Wedding ceremonies and baby showers are events that are closely attuned to our sense of tradition and well-being.

Perhaps one of the most profound rituals is found in death and loss. Specific actions are often called for in particular religions, including how services are conducted, types of urns or caskets used, musical selections, and burial rituals. In some societies, open weeping and wailing are expected. In others, behavior is much more sedate. These rituals can aid in alleviating grief, helping with closure, and, in some cultures, cement the belief in life after death.

Grief is a natural response to loss. The pain can be overwhelming whenever we lose someone or something we love. Our emotions can range from shock to anger to disbelief, even guilt and, of course, sadness. The pain can disrupt our sleep, eating, and ability to think and process or make decisions. These are normal reactions to our loss.

We usually associate grief with the death of a loved one, which can be the most difficult and trying experience in one's life. However, any loss or death can be extremely painful and life-altering.

Helpguide.org contains a wealth of information for those experiencing the pain of bereavement and loss. It points out that any loss can create sadness, shock, disbelief, guilt over past things you did or didn't do, feeling helpless and alone or lost, and fear or worries about the future.[4]

Loss can include any of the following:

- Divorce or the end of a relationship
- Loss of health
- Loss of a job
- Loss of financial stability
- A miscarriage
- Retirement
- Death of a pet
- Loss of a cherished dream
- A loved one's serious illness
- Loss of a friendship
- Loss of safety after a trauma
- The sale of the family home

Some losses are much more significant and difficult to bear. The loss of a spouse or partner can impact managing funeral arrangements and financial issues. You grieve for the loss of time together or have to explain the loss to your children.

The loss of a parent also represents a traumatic period. For children, this can present enormous adjustment issues. Even for adults, when a parent passes, even if they have been ill, we are reminded of our mortality. Now we are the older generation, and if your relationship wasn't an easy one, you could be left with guilt and conflicting emotions.

Perhaps one of the most difficult losses is losing a child. Our children are supposed to outlive us. No matter the age of the child, whether he is an infant or an adult, there remains a sense of "it's not right." Trying to come to terms with the loss can cause conflict and blame within a marriage. I've known of two couples who ultimately divorced after the death of a child. My sister lost her adult daughter

4. Smith, Melinda, Lawrence Robinson, and Jeanne Segal. 2021. "Coping with Grief and Loss." https://www.helpguide.org/articles/grief/coping-with-grief-and-loss.htm. HelpGuide.org, August. Accessed 29 September 2021.

to leukemia. When I asked her how she dealt with that, her reply surprised me. She said, "I believe that God lent her to us for a time for us to enjoy." This belief assisted her, and her husband relish the time they'd spent with their daughter while she was alive.

Suicide is another difficult loss. The shock can seem overwhelming. You might struggle for years to come to terms with that loss, especially if it was a child or an adolescent. I know a person who still struggles with her guilt and pain over a son's suicide a dozen years later.

Some people might minimize the death of a pet. But for others, a pet is a member of the family. The grieving process is no different than that following a human loss. For children who lose a pet, the experience can be traumatic. Parents and caregivers need to talk openly with the children and encourage them to share their sadness. Erecting a memorial or holding a service can aid in coping with the loss.

Regardless of the type of loss, managing your response is the key to future recovery and well-being. Accepting that your life will never be the same again is essential to healing. Recognize that all people manage their losses differently. There is no specific road, no certain time to grieve and heal.

In 1969 Elisabeth Kübler-Ross introduced the five stages of grief based on her studies of how patients faced terminal illness. These are denial, anger, bargaining, depression and acceptance. However, people do not have to go through these stages to heal. Some people can resolve their grief without going through any of these stages. We are all different.

Leaning on your support system and being with others who care offers further healing. Even rituals such as gathering together to tell silly, funny, or even sad stories can help commemorate a person's life and act as a catalyst to healing. Some people can use their routines, such as household duties, their children's needs, or their work to aid them in distraction from the pain and lead to finding peace and acceptance in their loss. Others rely on their rituals, their church family, the hymns of their childhood, prayer, and the rituals associated with closure at the funeral and cemetery services.

Rituals around personal loss, such as divorce or break-ups, can involve tearing up or burning photos. Other rituals include sports and competitions where participants wear certain shirts or hats as good luck charms. Often, we see this in celebrity figures who have their own set of rituals before games. Such rituals may be perceived as superstition. Others include such behaviors as throwing salt over one's shoulder or avoiding walking under a ladder. While these rituals or routines might seem useless, they can reduce anxiety and provide a sense of self-assurance.

Many personal rituals connected with spiritual beliefs can include reciting prayers before bedtime or repeating grace before meals, such as "God is great, God is good, and we thank Him for our food." Such rituals become part of family heritage, often continuing through many generations.

What happens without rituals, whether family, individual or societal? Typically, we lose the value or structure and routine in our lives, which provides a sense of security and safety. We recognize the importance of certain events and behaviors, and we trust that these will happen and that we can count on them. Why did many of us react so angrily and, yes, resentfully during COVID? Our structures, our rituals were suddenly pulled out from under us. Often it wasn't just that "they" took away our freedom. No, it went beyond that.

No longer could we have our weekly Saturday breakfast with friends in our favorite restaurant. We could no longer shake hands. We could not enjoy hot dogs and sodas with our friend at the ballpark. More importantly, we were no longer able to share holidays such as Christmas with family. The rituals had been yanked from us.

Routine and ritual represent stability and balance in our lives. Without them, we can flounder.

If you have not established a new balance in your life after COVID, I now encourage you to do so. Begin by examining your routine and that of your family. Start by simply listing your normal daily routine, the one that controls the rest of your activities. Appointments, special events, outside activities can all float around your normal routine. The morning routine probably begins with breakfast. If you have children, bedtime hours may vary, depending upon the child's age. Still, parents must stick to their rules to maintain routine except on special occasions. Children thrive much more easily in that environment. So do we all.

Some necessary activities can easily become part of a routine.

Others can be easily sandwiched in. The crucial factor is maintaining comfortable stability. Most of us dislike changes in our routines. We sometimes rebel when the boss asks us to work late. We may descend into sadness when someone we love is hospitalized and the stability is disrupted. Our fears climb the heights of our imagination. Not only has our routine been upset, but our family and social rituals have been interrupted. No wonder many of us have cursed COVID for its intrusion.

Describe your daily routines. What interruptions bother you the most? Can you recall a positive interruption? What about the worst interruption of your life? Ask yourself, how did you handle these times? What could you do differently?

Now, describe your family and personal rituals. Which ones provide the most meaning or pleasure in your life? Have you ever discarded a past ritual? If so, why? Or have you substituted a new one in its place?

As you review your daily and weekly activities, consider what drives your activities throughout the day or week. Are there specific changes you could make in your routines that might positively impact your life? Has your use of rituals positively impacted your life and enabled you to get through the pandemic more easily? As outlined in the next section, all of your behaviors and daily actions can connect with your goals and objectives.

14

Establishing Goals

Once you have established a steady routine, what is the next step in reshaping yourself? Perhaps you had dreams that you put on hold for the past months. Perhaps you have vices you'd love to conquer but no clue as to where to start. Maybe you are just breathing a huge sigh of relief—glad it appears over at last, even with variant strains of the virus. You may feel like you can return to whatever felt normal for you. Maybe you dread wading through the crowd of shoppers that block your access to the frozen lasagna. Perhaps you find your hands shaking at the thought of attending your company meeting. Maybe you are angry that your company requires you to get vaccinated to retain your job.

Yes, we are all in a different position now. You may find yourself forgetting to sanitize all your doorknobs and countertops. You may no longer be washing your hands a hundred times a day. You notice that many shoppers are not wearing their masks, and you feel comfortable now going without yours. Even when you hear news of the Delta or Omicron variants, you feel assured that the pandemic has peaked. You are now moving into your comfort zone, or you may be the person who is moving out of your comfort zone.

Comfort zones feel pleasant and safe. Yet, they can hinder us from making positive progress in our lives. You may have had a dream of becoming a licensed nurse or getting a welding certificate, but the thought of returning to school, studying, or the cost involved deterred you. Therefore, you may have elected to remain in your comfort zone—frozen in place. It's much easier to stay exactly where you are instead of taking a risk. The fear of failure and the fear of success are opposites, but oddly enough, either one can keep you from achieving your dreams.

To move forward in our personal or professional lives, we must move out of that comfort zone, which is not easy. Moving out of our comfort zone can be very difficult and even costly in terms of time and money. It can create anxiety at times and even fuel tension with family, friends, or co-workers. Any time we embark on a new course of action, it is often scary.

But as Christopher Robin says to Winnie the Pooh in the Disney film *Pooh's Grand Adventure*, "You're braver than you believe, stronger than you seem, and smarter than you think."

To be brave and strong does require a certain amount of smarts. Making changes and stepping out of the COVID adventure requires that we plan. And how do we do this? The answer is setting realistic goals. To do this, we must have a strategic plan. Compare this to driving to a family reunion. Aunt Mary resides in Phoenix, and you live in Denver. In today's computer world, you would type in the addresses, and the result would give you directions to the reunion site. In your grandmother's time, you would spread a map on the kitchen table and trace the journey using a black marker.

Whatever you do, you cannot reach the reunion site if you do not know where Aunt Mary lives. Our goals are much like that. We must know our destination to achieve positive results with our life plans. Perhaps one of the best methods to begin your journey is with a personal vision statement.

Sometimes the personal vision statement is known as a mission statement. Companies often use these for making basic and strategic decisions. For you, it can act as your guidance system and a reference point for all the decisions you make in life. You will be able to structure your goals specifically around your vision statement.

You may be wondering about how specific or how relevant such a statement should be. If you have never even considered, much less constructed one, you may not know where to begin. When asked in an interview what he hoped to achieve through his choice of roles, Australian actor Aaron Pedersen said he wanted to focus on the social issues of the Aboriginal people. Being of Aboriginal heritage, Pedersen is quite aware of the historic and even current barriers this indigenous population faces.

As you might gather from this example, a vision statement is fairly broad but acts as a guide. Dr. Martin Luther King, Jr., for example, might have had a personal statement that he sought a world where people are judged by their character and not the color of their skin.

Your statement might not be so vast. However, it should encompass your beliefs. As a teacher, you might want to bring to your students the value of education. That vision would, in turn, affect your daily lesson plans and presentations. As a social worker, your mission might be to protect all children. The result will be reflected in your daily interactions with neglected and abused children.

As you begin constructing your statement, the first consideration should be strategy. Then look at your map. How can you arrive at your destination, and what will be the result? What can you leave the world as a result of your accomplishment? What is your purpose? Your vision will also result in your ability to say "yes" or "no" as life presents options during your journey.

To create your vision statement, begin by focusing on the future, as in the examples above. Then, pick a direction. How does your statement coincide with the path you've chosen in life? If you are passionate about teaching, writing, computers, mechanics, accounting, music, acting or another pursuit, your mission needs to align with your direction.

Next, make your vision statement relevant for your life and society. Perhaps you have been the victim of domestic violence in a past relationship. Your vision might be "I want to ensure that no other woman ever suffers abuse at the hands of a partner." Then, you can establish your goals around this mission, giving time and funds and possibly setting up a support system to accomplish your purpose. You need a strong reason for following your purpose. Otherwise, you will lose your incentive. Your goals should be strongly aligned with your vision and require time and effort. However, at times, life gets in the way, and you may decide, "Oh, well, it isn't worth it anyway."

Please include your core values and beliefs as you draft your statement and strive to create a rewarding experience for yourself. You need to receive a benefit. Perhaps you are counseling a man who went on a binge this past weekend. Your reward is that you felt as if you did something worthwhile and impacted his life. Don't forget that your statement must also be challenging and inspire you and others.

As you draft your vision, be certain it is clear and concise, simple. Avoid jargon or vague phrases. Have a timeline in mind, a finish line. Remember that you arrived at your Aunt Mary's for the family reunion by following your map. Life contains many diversions and options. By charting your course with a clear statement, you can avoid detours. Perhaps your vision included a value that all people should read and comprehend the meaning of words. Therefore, you incorporated that vision into your teaching career goals.

A good personal vision statement does several things:

It keeps you on track.
It helps you push through times of laziness.
It provides something you can cling to when fear comes.
It gives you a feeling of pride when you see it manifested in the world.[1]

Now that you have developed a vision statement, what is the next step? First of all, ask yourself "What is a goal?" Psychologist and career coach Erin Eatough explains that a goal is simply something you want to achieve. It's the desired result that you or a group of people plan and commit to achieving. Set a goal with a deadline.[2]

Goals should help us reach our personal statement. They should motivate us and set us up for success. We need to focus on SMART goals:

- Specific
- Measurable
- Attainable
- Relevant
- Time-bound

Open your journal and write down your goals. Writing down your goals makes them more tangible, and you might even post them on the refrigerator for easy visibility and as a reminder. Break your goals down into steps that can guide you to success. Perhaps your

1. Wright, Brian. 2021. "What Is a Personal Vision Statement?" The Life Synthesis, September 8. https://thelifesynthesis.com/personal-vision-statement-examples. Accessed September 26, 2021.
2. Eatough, Erin. 2021. "How to Set Goals and Achieve Them: 10 Strategies for Success." Better Up, July 15. https://www.betterup.com/blog/how-to-set-goals-and-achieve-them. Accessed September 26, 2021.

goal is to stop smoking completely by December 31 this year. With the support of your family, your counselor, and your medical advisor, this goal may be possible. However, if you stop this day, it may be impossible to refrain from purchasing another pack. Instead decide that you can smoke one less cigarette each day for the next two weeks. Once you are successful, you drop two more cigarettes per day and so forth until you find that you are smoking two packs less each week. By breaking down your goal, you can feel more successful and that your goal is indeed attainable.

How many goals should you have? I urge caution, especially on long-term goals. If your current list is to stop smoking by the end of the year, lose thirty pounds by that time, and quit biting your fingernails, you are going to fail. Make priorities. You decide to work on smoking for health reasons. The other two goals move down the list. As you gain success in abstinence, you may find that you are eating better and maybe your anxiety level has decreased. Your nails are a bit longer.

Along the way, don't forget Plan A and Plan B. Life gets messy at times. Our best-laid plans can go astray. As you began your internship in social work, you discovered that you disliked the constant interaction with people, with rules and processes. You can't sleep at night; your nerves are shot. You remember how you loved numbers and begin checking out the possibilities of switching to an accounting degree. Plan A and Plan B are important, along with a reminder that we can always modify our plan and goals.

We need realistic goals, a series of them, moving from simple and small goals to short-term and long-term goals. Establishing your goals requires making a list of what you wish to achieve. What are your dreams, and what are the obstacles? On the surface, this may appear overwhelming, depending on your particular goal and the resources available. Breaking down your goals is critical, so you do not become discouraged from the start.

Mark Twain once said, "The secret of getting ahead is getting started."

To begin, make three columns and label them small goals, short-term goals, and long-term goals. At this point, jot one or several items under each goal.

Now focus on the small list. This list should be only for those specific mini goals that are doable in the next week. They are very short term. Your list could include items such as mailing a birthday card to your sister, walking around the block, buying dog food, washing the car, mowing the lawn. These might be routine duties, but you can easily put off doing them if you are not careful. The purpose of this small list is to set the pace. You cross them off your list as they are accomplished, which provides you with the incentive to continue. You gain confidence that you can complete even the most mundane and (sometimes) irritating tasks. Yes, sometimes you may have to push yourself into action. Surely the lawn can wait another week. But then, when you see and smell the lawn after you put the mower back into the shed, you feel that satisfying sense of completion.

Short-term goals enable you to pick up the pace. These are goals that you might be able to accomplish perhaps in the next three months to a year. Are there some simple tasks here that might be moved to the small goal list? Perhaps picking up that job application could happen today. If you spot such goals, feel free to move them over to the small goals list. Short-term goals should be more serious. Examples might include "I will smoke one less cigarette every day for the rest of the month and then drop to two less"; "I want to complete one basic class toward my nursing degree this quarter"; "I will repay my court fines by this date." Your short-term goals are yours alone and not dictated by anyone else, even if you have other demands.

Keep in mind that short-term goals can build into your long-term goals. An example of a short-term goal for a writer might be "Write one chapter every day," whereas the long-term goal is to complete the novel within twelve months. For the student, the short-term goal is to complete a class that semester. The long-term might be graduating with a master's degree in psychology.

Long-term goals move us into the completion of specific life purposes. Examples might include "I will remain clean and sober for the rest of my life"; "I will use my sociology degree to work with homeless people"; or "I will be able to purchase a home for my family." Achieving these goals requires short-term preparation. They require work and stick-to-itiveness, and some people drop out. Others change their goals.

One patient told me of her dream to be a nurse. But as she progressed with her classes, she reached a stumbling block. She did not like drawing blood or sticking people with needles. She became ill and agitated each time she had to go through these procedures with her supervisor. Eventually, she dropped the idea and decided to work on a business degree.

We can change our minds at any point. When we get more information and experience, realize ourselves and recognize our purpose and what appears to drive our initiative, we can alter our course. I encourage you not to consider the time to be wasted if this happens to you. One person said exactly that. "I lost a whole semester because I made a bad choice."

I asked her to reframe that. What did you learn this semester? Who did you meet? What made you decide to seek a new course? Her time and energy were not misspent. As it turned out, she discovered a new field in which she could shine.

Yes, goals can push us forward, provide us with a sense of achievement, and perhaps develop into a lifetime commitment. A lot like a marriage, wouldn't you say? When you examine it from that point of view, isn't it like relationships, where we start with the small goal? Getting to meet a person. Our short-term goal is date a while to see if we are compatible. Maybe we can move in together. Long-term, let's commit, maybe marriage. Do all relationships and marriages work out? Of course not, but with hard work and devotion, the possibility exists.

Objectives are measurable and achievable activities. But goals require that we set specific objectives, or the likelihood of success fades. By using measurements that are observable, we can better ensure that we carve out the path toward completion. In addition, if we examine our strengths and abilities, we can establish objectives around those qualities.

For example, suppose your long-term goal is to purchase a new car. Can you break this down into small segments? If you are working, you could save $20 from each paycheck and put it into a separate account. That is an actual measurable goal. For how long? Each week for the next year. While this amount may not be enough for a new car, perhaps it will make a down payment.

Perhaps you desire to teach school children—a worthy goal. How can you achieve this? Small goals might include printing out a college admissions form or applying for a student loan. When? Set a date. By the end of the week. Your longer goal may be finish two classes each semester. You've set a date. From that start, you complete one year, then two. As you can see, as you finish each segment and meet smaller goals and measurable objectives, you will be able to begin student teaching and, eventually, have your classroom of second graders!

The challenge that often holds us back occurs when we examine the "big picture." I'll never be able to buy that car. It's too expensive. I won't be able to get a loan, and I have too many other expenses. We often give up.

The other challenge is that we become overwhelmed. We make excuses. It will take too long to get a degree. I won't get a student loan. I'll end up with too much debt. I won't be able to get a good job anyway. We give up. If we start the process and move forward, meeting each objective with determination, we are encouraged by success. And yes, those smaller successes act as an incentive.

Objectives work secondarily as well. If you are the person who felt imprisoned during the pandemic, you can manage your frustration by setting goals for managing your emotions. You can set objectives for yourself, such as better reducing your anxiety this week from ten out of ten to six out of ten. By playing these games with yourself, you can instill calmness and peace in your mind.

The same concept works if you are the person who feels fearful about attending your first all-staff meeting. You can examine your relaxation skills, training yourself in advance to lower your anxiety from a ten out of ten to a seven out of ten. Using some of the skills presented in this book, you can practice relaxation and mindfulness tools so that you do not panic during such events.

Your life may have changed considerably since the beginning of the pandemic. The good news is that you have been able to find a measure of stability and self-assurance by using your strengths, despite COVID variants and the introduction of vaccination policies for returning to work. To further your journey to security and contentment, you must now focus on continual self-care and growth.

15

Finding Harmony

COVID-19 and its variants have left a lot of sand and seaweed in its wake. Our beaches are strewn with debris from the tidal waves. But you do not have to wade through the mess alone. Each of us can reach out to others and together find the pearls that sparkle in the aftermath.

To reach out to interact with others positively and compassionately, you must focus on self-care. Discovering the tools, exercises and skills that work for you is critical in this process. By using these appropriate tools, you can achieve a sense of balance in your life.

Maintaining balance in your life often is a challenge. You may follow all the suggestions and exercises in this book and still find yourself struggling at times. Life is chaotic. Life is often unexpected; just look at late 2019 and early 2020. Few of us predicted that a contagion known as COVID would throw a blanket over our plans. You may have breathed a sigh of relief with the introduction of vaccines. Some of your co-workers had different views, and others felt angry when they heard of the possibility of vaccine mandates. Because you already had your vaccine and were again working in your office, you weren't particularly concerned about the changes.

But then you noticed that the mandates were affecting your workplace. You learned that federal employees and contractors must show proof of vaccination with no testing option. With the new mandates, about 80 million workers now had a choice between providing proof of vaccination or submitting to weekly COVID testing. Because your clinic receives Medicaid and

Medicare funding, all the workers now face the mandate and must be vaccinated.[1]

One of your co-workers was incensed and said he was going to "sue someone." He'd heard of several police officers who were suing their department or state because they didn't think anyone had the right to tell them what to do. One of your friends works as a courier, and because her company has over one hundred employees, it required her to be vaccinated. If she isn't, she can't do any medical runs.

As you read further, you learn that cities, states, and employers can require vaccination or testing in place of vaccination. While some of your co-workers continue to express contempt for the regulations, you review the progress that you have made in bouncing back from COVID. Although you can't change others, you can demonstrate the skills you have learned throughout the pandemic. You also continue to reach out to sustain balance by embracing other tools.

Life can be relentless and bring us heartache, pain, and grief. These are the moments when we need to reach beyond ourselves. We need to rely on our medical and mental health resources.

After you have connected with your medical provider and received a clean bill of health or instructions on maintaining this fabulous machine that is your body, follow her advice. Then consider connecting with a counselor, therapist, spiritual advisor, psychologist or psychiatrist. If you are uncertain how to proceed, ask your medical professional for a referral or suggestions. You also can go online and check the credentials, experience, education, and even any complaints against the person before making a decision.

How do you determine which mental health provider is best for you? First of all, knowing your major complaint will help. Your teenage son sneaking out at night will probably require a very different approach than you will if your mother just died. Perhaps you served in the military in the Middle East and experience nightmares and flashbacks.

---

1. Mendez, Rich. 2021. "What You Need to Know About President Joe Biden's New Covid Vaccine Mandates." CNBC, September 10. www.cnbc.com/2021/09/10/what-yu-need-to-know-about-President-Joe-Biden's-new-Covid-vaccine-mandates.html. Accessed 22 September 2021.

You can schedule an appointment with a provider to determine if the two of you will be a good fit. Your personalities or styles may not be compatible. At the first session, I try to tell my patients that they can change providers if they do not feel comfortable. They can change at any point during therapy. Finally, I will readily refer them to another clinician to get the best treatment for their particular problems.

Finally, a key determination is the type of therapy a provider offers or specializes in. There are many different approaches to treatment. One size does not fit all. A brief examination of the different types of therapy may act as a guide as you refine your search to meet your needs.

Cognitive behavioral therapy (CBT): This goal-oriented approach focuses on changing negative and maladaptive thoughts into positive and productive ones. Developed by Aaron Beck, who had practiced psychoanalysis, CBT focuses on identifying negative, unhelpful thoughts and modifying your behaviors. For example, if you fear that the COVID vaccine will kill you, a therapist who specializes in CBT can help you examine your fears. By processing your thoughts with existing data, you may be able to overcome this belief.

CBT is used often to help people who exhibit anxiety, stress, depression and phobias. Sometimes it is used to help modify habits, such as smoking, overeating, or gambling.

Dialectical behavior therapy (DBT): DBT is a modified type of CBT. Originally, it was intended to treat borderline personality disorder but has been adapted to treat other mental health conditions, such as emotional regulation, post-traumatic stress disorder (PTSD), and eating and substance use disorders.

A key to treatment is using mindfulness tools, extensively referenced in several portions of this book. Other keys include distress tolerance and interpersonal effectiveness. Strategies include self-acceptance and collaboration with your support team. DBT is often used in many settings, such as individual or group therapy, in person or over the phone or via video chat.

Psychodynamic or psychoanalysis therapy: This type of therapy examines the unconscious meanings of and motivations for behaviors, thoughts, and feelings. Psychoanalysis was first developed by Sigmund Freud, who believed that uncovering the unconscious roots of a person's symptoms could help them live a more contented life. This therapy can also help people interact and communicate with others more effectively. In addition, it is frequently used to manage life changes, such as having a new baby, retiring, and caring for elderly parents.

Humanistic therapy: This therapeutic approach emphasizes that people can make rational choices and develop their potential. Several subtypes of therapy fall under the humanistic branch, including client-centered, Gestalt, and existential therapy.

Client-centered therapy focuses on the idea that therapists are not "the boss" but are there to help their clients change by demonstrating therapeutic concern, care, and interest. Gestalt emphasizes the importance of being aware of the "here and now" and accepting personal responsibility. The existential approach focuses on free will, self-determination, and the search for meaning.

The humanistic approach in its various forms can be used to treat depression, anxiety, panic disorders, personality disorders, schizophrenia, addiction, and relationship issues. People with low self-esteem might benefit from this approach as they search for personal meaning. Talk therapy is used to identify past events affecting the patient's well-being.

Solution-based therapy: This is a short-term, goal-focused approach focused on solutions rather than the problems that brought clients to therapy. This brief therapy offers an approach to situations that may be practical. For example, if the patient reports he is unemployed, the therapist might ask a "miracle question": "How will your life be different if a miracle occurs?" This strategy opens the door to generate questions that can lead patients to solve their problems.

Like most types of therapy, solution-based therapy can aid in various problems but focuses more on those issues that don't require long-term treatment. As a result, many clients find results more quickly and with less intrusion into their history. It is a practical model in criminal justice, child welfare, domestic violence treatment, and education.

In addition to the above primary therapy methods, several other types of treatment have evolved to focus on specific diagnoses and needs of patients. These treatment approaches are briefly mentioned here as a guide only. If you believe that you might benefit from any specific approach, you will want to discuss it with your therapist or medical provider.

All therapeutic approaches require that the provider receives education, practicums, experience, and specialized training. However, for the following, even more specific training is required. By examining all available information, you can determine the effectiveness for you. Keep in mind the importance of any cautionary information.

Exposure therapy: This approach is often used to help people confront their fears, ranging from panic disorder, social anxiety disorder, obsessive-compulsive disorder, PTSD, or generalized anxiety disorder. This procedure involves facing the feared object, either directly or indirectly. A person fearful of crowds could be expertly guided to integrate a shopping experience into his life in a non-fearful manner.

Aversion therapy: This approach changes pleasant feelings gained from negative habits and behaviors so the patient can recognize their negative impact. A person who is addicted to smoking, for example, will use this type of therapy and may feel ill or threatened by a cigarette.

Hypnotherapy: This approach uses hypnosis to achieve a change in the habits of the client. Those can range from smoking to weight control. Hypnotherapy can be used in childbirth and to treat bulimia and irritable bowel syndrome. This process is not to be confused with stage or entertainment hypnosis.

Eye movement desensitization (EMDR): The therapist uses finger or hand movements to guide the client's eyes from side to side to produce feelings of calm and control. It is used to treat addictions, eating disorders, panic attacks and anxiety. Some experts debate its effectiveness.

Reaching out to a qualified, licensed therapist may provide additional support as you move beyond COVID-19 to renewed stability and purpose. With the fluctuations of the pandemic from its beginning until now, maintaining balance in your daily life should be a priority.

Balance refers to stability and bringing yourself into harmony. You might think of it like a circus performer on a high wire. He steps cautiously and carefully navigates across the wire, balancing himself with a pole. When he feels a breeze threatening to topple him, he adjusts the pole, maintaining his position until he reaches his goal.

We, too, must use our poles for balance. We need to rely on our resources as we move through life to maintain our balance. Breezes blow across our path. Storms threaten to destroy what we have achieved. To ward off possible destruction, we must use our tools to sustain our equilibrium.

Have you completed your bucket list? You may have heard the term tossed around a lot, especially on television and in the movies. You probably have a basic idea of what is meant by this term. You may even have a laugh or two at two old, terminally ill men living out their dreams and last days together. But did you realize the serious message?

"Bucket list" comes from the phrase "kicking the bucket." As long as you're checking off items on that list, that means you are alive and healthy, according to www.theodysseyonline.com/why-its-good-have-bucket-list.

The American Heritage Dictionary says the term bucket list derives from the French, loosely meaning an obstacle course. Yes, life can be an obstacle course at times.

But perhaps the first usage, as we now understand it, was in the 2003 book *Unfair & Unbalanced: The Lunatic Magniloquence of Henry E. Paky* by Patrick M. Carlisle. Carlisle writes, "who doesn't want to go gently into the blacky black night. He wants to cut loose, dance on the razor's edge, pry the lid off his bucket list!"

Since then, the term bucket list has indicated things we would like to do before we die. The dreams we have, the places we'd like to visit, and our career ambitions often fall short for many of us. At times, our work, daily activities, and circumstances seemingly beyond our control play a large part. Why?

COVID-19 has provided a clear message. Some of you may have lost family or friends to the virus. Some of you may still be recovering or suffering long-lasting effects. The bucket list is a solid reminder that our time on Earth is limited, a reminder of our mortality.

How many of us have heard the laments: "Betty and I always wanted to go to Ireland, but work got in the way." "I always meant to call Mike again, let him know how much I appreciated him at my bedside, but I just got busy." For too many people, it takes a terrifying illness, a major life change like retirement, or some other major event to honestly be thinking about all the things we want to do before we die.[2]

For many people, it can be too late to turn our dreams into reality. Life is uncertain. We only have to look back on the beginnings of COVID-19 to recognize that fact. Some of our travel dreams, our vacation plans, our reunions were all postponed. The other consideration is our health. In ten years or twenty, we may not be able physically, emotionally, or financially to participate in certain activities.

For many years, I dreamed of traveling to Ireland. It was at the top of my bucket list. Yet, work, money, and fear all seemingly stood in the way. Then, three years ago, my oldest granddaughter treated me to a trip! So, thanks to her frequent-flyer miles and hotel credits, off we flew to a very memorable two weeks in Europe. My only regret—my aching legs.

Before leaving, I received injections from my doctor. Nevertheless, my total pleasure was limited. The journey required much walking. For example, I could not walk to the top of the hill for a complete overview of Giant's Causeway. Yes, I had an excellent view, but climbing and walking would have been less intense if I had traveled two or three years earlier.

My message is to follow your bucket list. There is no perfect time. Engaging in the activities we enjoy and following our dreams enriches our life and health.

To begin your bucket list, author Vanessa Van Edwards recommends that you "dreamstorm," a combination of dreaming and brainstorming.[3] Take out a piece of paper or open a new document on your computer and set aside at least fifteen minutes to put your ideas into writing. Let your mind roam free. Write down every idea that pops into your head. It doesn't matter how logical or fantastic it may seem. Just write and do not edit at this time; let your brain run free.

When the time is up, begin to break down the ideas. Some will

---

2. White, Annette. n.d. "How to Make a Bucket List: 5 Easy Steps to Create a Great One." https://buckewtlistjourney.net/how-to-make-a-bucket-list. Accessed September 25, 2021.

3. Van Edwards, Vanessa. n.d. "The Ultimate Guide to Creating Your Bucket List Right Now." Science of People. https://www.scienceofpeople.com/bucket-list. Accessed September 25, 2021.

grab your attention almost instantly. This sorting process can also be applied to looking at the goals you may have set in the last chapter. You can classify your bucket list ideas into categories: seasons, years, or decades. Select the top three. These are the dreams that you are going to turn into reality. Don't worry about or feel overwhelmed by the process. Just examine what excites you the most and what has a time limit.

After that, ask yourself several questions.

- Who: Is this your goal alone, or is someone joining you?
- When: When does it need to happen? What time of day? Get specific.
- Where: Where do you need to go and how to get there?
- How: How do you complete this goal? How much money do you need?
- What: What do you need to make this happen? What is the first step?

The next step is to select the number one item and make that your priority. Be as specific as possible and anticipate any problems so when the time comes to make memories, you can focus on enjoying the moment. In addition, remember that your bucket list is not to be completed. You may add items to the list and check off other items as they have been completed.

Today, this very day, as you read this, I would like you to make a bucket list in your journal. Write down at least three items you would like to accomplish in your life. Prioritize them into categories of family, friends, and self. Perhaps you would like to reconnect with a child. Maybe you'd like to take your bride of thirty years to Hawaii or finish writing that novel you started in college. Whatever your list may be, you owe it to yourself and to the people around you to complete at least one item on your list within the next year or six months. *You* should set a reachable goal and follow through.

Begin with those personal values discussed earlier. How did you feel when you focused on the positive values? Can you recall a time when you let yourself down and made bad decisions or choices? Comparing the difference in your emotions, you may seem more pleased with your life when you focus on the good or morally correct values. You want to bring those values to the forefront when you are faced with personal dilemmas. By doing so, you will find more peace and contentment in your life.

Perhaps in your list of values, you considered gratitude. We often forget the profound impact that gratitude has on our lives and the lives of others. Simple ways of demonstrating your thanks and appreciation can promote pleasant feelings and sometimes cement relationships. Gratitude is often used in mindfulness exercises by instilling positive mood changes. There is evidence-based research that indicates that it can be used to alleviate mild to moderate depression.

Gratitude is expressed in simple acts of appreciation and kindness and attention to what's important in our daily existence. It can be as basic as smiling at someone. We often get preoccupied with daily routines. We fail to note those people and things that complement our well-being. Take a few moments out of the day to express your gratitude to others. Recognizing how fortunate we are brings joy and pleasure into our lives.

Melody Beattie in *Gratitude* reminds us that we should express gratitude for the ordinary in our lives. The sun rises each morning, and the seasons come and go with regularity. We forget how miraculous and awesome these ordinary events are. Standing outside on a starry night, breathing the air while we enjoy the marvelous expanse of beauty above us, evokes a magical quality of gratitude. Or we might just feel grateful that we have running water or electricity and lights. Some people do not. We have food in our refrigerator. Some do not.

On the other side, being grateful for what we do not have is equally important. If you have never had an addiction or a serious mental health issue or physical illness, this is certainly something to be thankful for. We also can be thankful for programs that help support the homeless and those who provide treatment or financial support for the needy.

Thankfulness and gratefulness are linked closely. We often associate thankfulness with the holiday Thanksgiving. Families and friends gather for a meal and may often recite a blessing before dining. They may have a traditional prayer or ritual to celebrate their gratitude for the yearly event. With the pandemic in 2020, many families were unable to gather for this holiday and others. Some may have felt angry about this intrusion into their personal choices. Now is the time to express your thankfulness for family, loved ones, and the blessings of a roof over our head, running water, and electricity.

As you continue to revitalize yourself after COVID, you may find that a mantra provides daily inspiration. What is a mantra? Originally from Hinduism or Buddhism, a mantra is a word or sound to aid concentration or meditation. For most of us today, it is simply a slogan or statement that is important to us. The word mantra stands for *man* or mind while *tra* is transport. Thus, your mantra can be used as a vehicle to move your mind from the tsunami of COVID and its aftermath to a harmonious landscape.

A mantra is simply a statement, a belief, or encouraging words that have special meaning for you. It could be a Biblical passage. Many examples of mantras exist, but you must discover one for yourself or create your own. A few inspiring words spoken to yourself, perhaps whispered or visualized in your mind, can inspire you as you undertake this marvelous adventure called life.

A few examples of mantras for your consideration:

Today will be a great day.
I feel blessed today.
My body is a miracle.
I love my life.
I am confident in my choices.
I listen to my heart.
I believe in love.
My spirit is at peace.

You may have a more appropriate mantra formed from your life experiences. Perhaps you use a family saying or something someone who has inspired you over the years has said. It might also be recalling a personal experience that changed your life. Some people find that a simple sound spoken aloud creates a sense of peace within them. I urge you to seek your mantra today!

Anxiety and depression can come from many sources. Whether a personal problem, such as loss of job, or something as simple as a traffic ticket, or a major disaster or pandemic such as COVID and its variants, the stressors can seem to overwhelm you. Have you ever wished that you could magically retreat to a happy place?

Also known as a safe place, this ideal spot should be special for you. It is your spot where you can retreat at a moment's notice. No one is allowed to enter. You can retreat there in your mind—safe from all the cares and problems of the world.

You can rely on visualization or a mindful exercise to restore calm to your spirit and relax. Can you recall a special place from your childhood or another location that provided that sense of peace and contentment? Perhaps it was a mountain, a special room, or another place. Visualize this scene in your mind. Remember, as in all mindful exercises, use all your senses for the most effective result.

Now begin to create the image more powerfully by using each of your senses. Visualize the colors of the various components, the deep greens, the blazing yellow sun, the fleecy white clouds above. If you are in a room, do the same; describe your colors.

Next, *listen*. What are the various sounds? Birds? Music? A soft breeze whistling through the trees?

Smell. Try to describe the smells around you. The sweetness of new-mown grass? The smell of old books?

Touch. Feel the grass under your feet. Touch the smooth book cover.

Taste. Yes, allow yourself to taste the leaf in your hand. Lightly lick the edge of a bookshelf or another object in the room.

As you perform each of these actions, take a few seconds to allow your senses to truly enjoy what you have housed in the memory of your happy or safe place. For full effect, journal your responses so that you can etch them more deeply in your mind.

Remind yourself that you can go to this place anytime you like—for a few brief seconds—even during a board meeting or while trying to diffuse a family argument. You can retreat to another room and enter your safe place for an extended period if you like.

Think of your happy or safe place as a gift to yourself, something you can rely on when the world goes crazy around you. Enjoy these precious moments.

As you move into life without COVID-19, by examining your mind, body, and spirit, you can adapt positively to whatever changes life brings. By engaging in ongoing self-assessment, using the tools that work for you, along with your support team and personal values, you will be able to manage yourself successfully. Reach out for professional help if needed. Continue to remind yourself that it is not the momentary situation, such as COVID-19 or any other personal event that controls your emotions and activities, but how you respond. These tools offer you the opportunity to enjoy a balanced life filled with contentment and harmony.

Continue your journey because it is your journey alone as you bounce back from COVID. Just remember that we are all works in progress, constantly in a state of growth. Enjoy and embrace this adventure known as life!

Additional Resources and Reading

Aasved, Mikal J. 2002. *The Psychodynamics and Psychology of Gambling: The Gambler's Mind.* Gambling Theory and Research Series, Vol. 1. Springfield, IL: Charles C. Thomas.

"The Adolescent Brain: Beyond Raging Hormones." 2005. National Library of Medicine, July. https://pubmed.ncbi.nlm.nih.gov/16193561/. Accessed 11 September 2021.

Alcoholics Anonymous. 2002. *Twelve Steps and Twelve Traditions.* New York: AA World Service.

Altman, Donald. 2014. *The Mindfulness Toolbox.* Eau Claire: PESI Publishing & Media.

Amatenstein, Sherry. 2020. "Sex Addiction: Signs, Symptoms, and Treatment." Psycom.net, 6 November. https://www.psycom.net/authors/sherry-amatenstein. Accessed 17 September 2021.

American Psychiatric Association. 2013. *Diagnostic and Statistical Manual of Mental Disorder: Fifth Edition.* Washington, D.C.: American Psychiatric Publishing.

Association for Spiritual, Ethical, and Religious Values in Counseling. n.d. https://servic.org/spiritual-and-religious-competencies/. Accessed 22 September 2021.

Beattie, Melody. 2007. *Gratitude.* Center City, MN: Hazelden.

Beck, Aaron, Gary Emery, and Ruth L. Greenberg. 2005. *Anxiety Age Disorder and Phobias: A Cognitive Perspective.* New York: Basic Books.

Binder, Carolyn Sue. 1995. *Albert Ellis: Dogmatic Christianity Detracts from and Disables Individual Growth and Development.* California: California State University Dominquez Hills.

Binder, Sue. 2007. *Hands Down: A Domestic Violence Treatment Book.* Alexandria: American Correctional Association.

Brick, John, and Carlton Erikson. 1999. *Drugs, the Brain, and Behavior: The Pharmacology of Abuse and Dependence.* New York: The Haworth Medical Press.

Brown, Helen. 2021. "26 Best Stress-Relief Techniques According to Psychology." Positive Psychology, 14 August. https://positivepsychology.com/stress-relief-techniques. Accessed on 17 September 2021.

Cashwell, C.S. and J.S. Young. 2020. *Integrating Spirituality and Religion into Counseling: A Guide to Competent Practice,* 3rd ed. Alexandria: American Counseling Association.

Cioals, Jessica. 2017. "Rosary Bead." Everyday Health, 15 November. https://www.everydayhealth.com/healthy-living/meaning-rosary-beads. Accessed 28 September 2021.

Cohen, Irvin A. 2021. *Fighting Covid-19, the Unequal Opportunity Killer: You Are Not Helpless in the Face of the Covid-19 Epidemic.* Topeka: Center for Health Information.

Cornelius, Gary. 2005. *Stressed Out: Strategies for Living and Working with Stress in Corrections.* Durham: Carolina Academic Press.

Additional Resources and Reading

Covey, Stephen R. 1989. *The 7 Habits of Highly Effective People.* New York: Simon & Schuster Inc.

De Becker, Gavin. 1998. *The Gift of Fear.* New York: Little, Brown.

Eatough, Erin. 2021. "How to Set Goals and Achieve Them: 10 Strategies." Better Up, 15 July. https://www.betterup.com/blog/how-to-set-goals-and-achieve-them. Accessed 26 September 2021.

Ellis, Albert, and Raymond Chip Tafrate. 1998. *How to Control Your Anger Before It Controls You.* Secaucus: Carroll.

Equal Justice Initiative. 2021. "Covid-19's Impact on People in Prison." Equal Justice Initiative, 16 April. https://eji/org/news/covid-19s-impact-on-people-in-prison. Accessed 24 September 2021.

Erickson, Dan. n.d. "Routine: The Pros and Cons of the Same Old Thing." https://www.hipdiggs.com/routine. Accessed 27 September 2021.

Flanagan, Leo F., Jr. 2021. *Thriving in Thin Air: Developing Resilience in Challenging Times.* New Orleans: The Center for Resilience.

The Four Basic Styles of Communication. n.d. https://www.uky.edu/hr/sites/www.uky.edu.hr/files/wellness/images/Conf14_FourCommStyles.pdf. Accessed 13 September 2021.

Freeman, Arthur, and Rose DeWolf. 1990. *Woulda, Coulda, Shoulda: Overcoming Regrets, Mistakes, and Missed Opportunities.* New York: HarperCollins.

Gino, Francesa, and Michael I. Norton. 2013. "Why Rituals Work." *Scientific American,* 14 May. https: www.scientificamerican.com/article/why-rituals-work. Accessed 27 September 2021.

Gregory, Christina. 2021. "Internet Addiction Disorder." Psycom.net, May 6. https://www.psycom.net/iadcriteria.html. Accessed 21 September.

Herring, Tiana, and Emily Widra. 2021. "Just Over Half of Incarcerated People Are Vaccinated, Despite Being Locked in COVID-19 Epicenters." Prison Policy Initiative, 18 May https://www.prisonpolicy.org/virus-virusresponse.html. Accessed 24 September 2021.

Hoffman, Jeffrey A., Mim J. Landry, and Berry D. Caudill. 2015. *Living in Balance: Moving from a Life of Addiction to a Life of Recovery.* Center City, MN: Hazelden.

Jones, Angela, Daniel Cohen, Brick Johnstone, Dong Pil Yoon, Laura H. Schopp, Guiy McCormack, and James Campbell. 28 April 2015: 17(2): 135–152. Relationships Between Negative Spiritual Beliefs and Health Outcomes for Individuals with Heterogeneous Medical Conditions. *Journal of Spirituality in Mental Health.*

Kübler-Ross, Elisabeth. 1969. *On Death and Dying.* New York: Macmillan.

Kuhar, Michael. 2011. *The Addicted Brain: Why We Abuse Drugs, Alcohol and Nicotine.* Hoboken: Pearson FT Press.

LaRue, Sarah. 2021. "Everyone Is a Helper: Psychological First Aid & Strategies for Sustainability." Colorado Community Health Network, Denver, CO, 10 June.

Lieberman, Matthew D. 2013. *Social: Why Our Brains Are Wired to Connect.* New York: Crown.

Marczweski, Jane, aka Nightbirde. 2021. "It's Okay." Uploaded to YouTube, June 28, 2021.

Mendez, Rich. 2021. "What You Need to Know About President Joe Biden's New Covid Vaccine Mandates." CNBC, 10 September. www.Cnbc.com/2021/09/10/what-yu-need-to-know-about-President-Joe-Biden's-new-Covid-vaccine-mandates.html. Accessed 22 September 2021.

Neil, Jennifer. "Domestic Violence and Covid-19: Our Hidden Epidemic." *Australian Journal of General Practice* 49 (June 11). https://www1.racgp.org.au/ajgp/coronavirus/domestic-violence-and-covid-19.

New York Times. 2021. "Coronavirus in the U.S.: Latest Map and Case Count." 16 April. https://nyti.ms/39/jvVJE. Accessed 24 September 2021.

Pelayo, Rafael. 2020. *How to Sleep.* Muskogee: Artisan.

Reiley, Laura. 2021. "The Cold Truth About Hot Lunch: School Meal Programs Are Running Out of Food and Workers." *Washington Post,* September 29.

Restak, Richard. 1994. *Receptors.* New York: Bantam.
Roth, Geneen. 1992. *When Food Is Love.* New York: Plume.
Rothenbuhler, Eric W. 1998. *Ritual Communication.* Newbury Park, CA: Sage Publshing.
Rouse, Scott. 2021. *Understanding Body Language.* Emeryville, CA: Rockridge Press.
Ruden, Ronald A., and Marcia Byaleck. 2000. *The Craving Brain.* New York: HarperCollins.
Schiraldi, Glenn R. 2001. *The Self-Esteem Workbook.* Oakland, California: New Harbinger Publications Inc.
Schwartz, Jeffrey, and Rebecca Gladding. 2012. *You Are Not Your Brain.* New York: Avery.
Singh, Shweta, et al. 2020. "Impact of COVID-19 and Lockdown on Mental Health of Children and Adolescents: A Narrative Review with Recommendations." Psychiatry Research 293 (November).
Smith, Melinda, Lawrence Robinson, and Jeanne Segal. 2021. *Coping with Grief and Loss.* HelpGuide.org, August. https://www.helpguide.org/articles/grief/comping-with-grief-and-loss.htm. Accessed 29 September 2021.
Spagnola, Mary, and Barbara H. Fiese. 2007. "Family Routines and Rituals: A Context for Development in the Lives of Young Children." *Infants & Young Children* 20(4): 284–299. https://journals.lww.com/lycjournal/Fulltext/2007/10000/Family-Routines. Accessed 28 September 2021.
Tarrant, Jeff. 2017. *Meditation Interventions to Rewire the Brain.* Eau Claire: PESI Publishing & Media.
Traylor, Jeff, with Inmate Zeno. 2004. *The Epictetus Club.* Huron, OH: Drinian Press.
Trimpey, Jack. 1996. *Rational Recovery: The New Cure for Substance Addiction.* New York: Gallery Books.
Van der Kolk, Bessel A., Alexander C. McFarlane, and Lars Weisaeth, Eds. 1996. *Traumatic Stress.* New York: Guilford Press.
Van Edwards, Vanessa. n.d. "The Ultimate Guide to Creating Your Bucket List Right Now." Science of People. https://www.scienceofpeople.com/bucket-list. Accessed 25 September 2021.
White, Annette. n.d. "How to Make a Bucket List: 5 Easy Steps to Create a Great One." Bucket List Journey by Annette. https://bucketlistjourney.net/how-to-make-a-bucket-list. Accessed 25 September 2021.
Wingfield, Debra. 2007. *Transformational Journaling for Recovering Souls.* Pueblo West, CO: Wingfield House of Peace Publishing.
Wright, Brian. 2021. "What Is a Personal Vision Statement?" The Life Synthesis, 8 September. https://thelifesynthesis.com/personal-vision-statement-examples. Accessed 26 September 2021.

Index

Index

Index

Index